Tabernacle

Unlocking the Secrets of Extravagant Worship and Prayer

Robin and Claire Dillamore

Freedom Publishing
Grieves Cottage, Drumelzier Haugh Farm
Broughton
Biggar ML12 6JD
United Kingdom

The right of the authors to be identified as the authors of this work has been asserted by them in accordance with the Copyright, Designs and Patents Act 1988.

A catalogue record for this book is available from the British Library

ISBN: 9781908154446

Front cover design by Cat Davis, madebycat.co.uk
Back cover by Esther Kotecha, EKDesigns
Typeset by Angela Selfe
Printed and bound in the UK

DEDICATION

This book is dedicated to our children
and grandchildren.

We hope that it forms part of a legacy
of which you can be proud.

We love you more than we can say.

CONTENTS

ENDORSEMENTS

Robin and Claire Dillamore both radiate the peace, joy and life of Christ wherever they go. This powerful book tells their testimony of discovering new expressions of worship that are rooted in the ancient story of the people of God. Like King David, they are people after God's heart who prioritise their lives around giving him the most extravagant praise.

The book shares their journey through the biblical story of day and night worship, and their own personal walk into greater freedom and dedication to seeing the name of Jesus lifted up. We are so inspired by their commitment to gathering worshippers not just to sing together but to build family around the presence of God. Robin and Claire are a gift to the community of Christ and we love them dearly!

Rich Di Castiglione
UK Director, David's Tent

Tabernacle is a book which, I believe, not only reflects God's heart, but also takes us on a process that leads us into a lifestyle of worship and intimacy. It is practical, biblical, inspirational and full of life and truth.

I love the way testimony and scripture are woven together to help us understand and identify with the truths being revealed. Put into practice, this book will change the way you live, and ultimately change the world you live in.

Sue Eldridge
Co-Director, Presence Ministries International and ELA

Tabernacle has been written by two amazing people. A couple that live and breathe the truths revealed in its pages, Robin and Claire have tapped into secrets of God that have been waiting for us to discover them. Not only have they tapped into them, they are outworking them in their own lives and in their city, seeing breakthrough and transformation. This book will take you on their journey, and bring you to a place where you, too, can learn to abide in His presence day and night.

Tim Eldridge
Co-Director, Presence Ministries International and ELA

I have met very few people that have both the passion and clarity on the subject of the Tabernacle of David like Robin and Claire. They have done a masterful job of weaving together their inspiring journey with very clear and revelatory teaching on the power of night and day worship and prayer. Their story will compel you to deeper places in God and give you blueprints for establishing places of His presence in the earth.

David Fritch
Author of *Enthroned: Bringing God's Kingdom to Earth through Unceasing Worship & Prayer*

Over the past few years it has been a privilege to get to know Robin and Claire and to now call them friends. Their love for Jesus and passion for worship is clear to see. Here in Chester, their desire to create a place and space for believers to gather together to draw near to

God, so they can express worship and intercession for extended times, has been a wonderful addition to the spiritual life of our city.

Reading their book helps you see the burden and desire that God has clearly put on their hearts to encourage extravagant worship and prayer. As you read through the chapters and reflect on the scriptures they lead us through, like us, your hearts will enlarge with a deeper passion for Jesus and for the transforming work of Holy Spirit in your life and city, town or village.

Andy and Sue Glover
Church Leaders within Chester
HBC Chester and Link Up

We just love Robin and Claire's passion, hunger and pursuit of deeper intimacy that oozes out of every chapter in this book. Their unfolding revelation of worship is so refreshing, moving and inspirational.

This book causes one to ask, 'God, give me a hunger and desire for You like I have never had before,' for they demonstrate that 'He satisfies the hungry with good things'.

These pages describe the compelling journey that Robin and Claire have embarked upon in their pursuit of intimacy and encounter with the living God. They take the fiery coals of passion from the altar of their hearts and freely offer them to the reader to be touched and transformed by the Holy and Burning One – Jesus Christ Himself!

Ian and Marj Rossol
Senior Leaders, All Nations Church, Leicester

Lord, we have heard of Your fame; we stand in awe of Your deeds, Lord. Repeat them in our day, in our time make them known.

(Habakkuk 3:2 NIV)

Speaking with humility, honesty and openness, Robin and Claire have invited us into their journey of intimacy with the Godhead, through abandoned worship and prayer. Their reason for telling their story is twofold: firstly, they want to show us steps we ourselves may take in response to the same invitation to intimacy that God extends to each one of us. Secondly, they want to show us the effect that moving in this way has on an individual, church, city and, ultimately, a nation.

As they have walked this journey, we have been privileged to have ringside seats. We have seen how they have lived the principles they have outlined, and we have seen the effect this has had on our city, as more and more people have caught what God is saying and doing. It has been an amazing journey, and there is still much, much more to come!!!

We would wholeheartedly recommend this book, for the many who are deeply hungry for the reality of the kingdoms of this world to become the Kingdom of our God.

Gerald and Lin Sidery
Senior Leaders, Northgate Church, Chester

Robin and Claire have truly unpacked depths of wisdom in this beautiful book on worship and prayer. They write with real humility as they share their personal journey including powerful visions and encounters with God, which makes this book hugely insightful as well as a gripping read! I am honoured to know Robin and Claire, and they are the 'real deal' – as I write this, they are leading 100 hours of worship and prayer in their city, and regularly hosting unity meetings with multiple church leaders.

This book is both a wonderful personal journey into a life of deep prayer and worship and a rich source of theology and revelation about the importance of night and day prayer and worship for the Church today. It unpacks the Biblical mandate to restore the 'Tabernacle of David', laying theological foundations with heartfelt passion. It explores details of theology from both the Old and New Testament, as well as fascinating history from the early Church. This book will excite for what God is doing on the earth today through worship and prayer, and release you into being a part of it!

JJ Waters
UK Director, Burn 24-7

FOREWORD

Jesus declared that His Father was seeking people who would worship in Spirit and Truth, free from constraints of physical location or religious ritual. God, the perfect, immeasurable, divine Spirit, wants spirit to Spirit worship that comes from the heart. True worship is glorious, mysterious, beyond description, direction or explanation. It is a response to His person, His presence, His love and His call for personal relationship. It is Spirit-inspired, Spirit-led and Spirit-empowered.

This book will speak to your spirit by the Spirit. Your mind will catch up later!

As your spirit is impacted through these words, you will find a longing to respond to the presence of God. You will probably stop reading at times and be drawn into worship. True worship.

We live in a time when desire for God's presence and a life centred on worship is a rapidly increasing phenomenon among Christians across the globe. It can be seen in many different expressions, as individuals and groups sacrificially respond to the wooing of the Holy Spirit. Worship starts and ends with God. It is not something we do; it is a response to relationship.

I have had the privilege of walking with Robin and Claire through part of their journey of faithful obedience as they transitioned from a 'normal Christian life' into a life of abandonment to God. They have learnt to trust God, be led into an increasingly intimate relationship with Him and also to live a life of worship in the mundane practicalities of life. It was a costly journey where they had to pay the price of choosing to live in this unfolding revelation, walking on an unknown path. It required courage and humility to allow God to challenge their understanding and, significantly, to challenge them to live in constant response to the Spirit, rather than organised and controlled by cultural habits or fear of man. But God, the Spirit of Truth, prepared them in advance for the journey and revealed Himself through His Word, convicting them of the necessary heart and lifestyle changes required to be true worshippers.

I honour them for being brave, open, honest and passionate, and especially for sharing the personal difficulties they faced.

This book is both apostolic and prophetic. It provides a scriptural foundation, revealing God's heart for relationship and how worship is integral to a true heart connection with Him. It also declares the faithfulness of God in pursuing us, ahead of our desire to pursue Him, and how He will lead us into His presence as we hear and respond.

Be aware! As you read this book you will be challenged, convicted and frustrated. That is a good thing. Let this book be a provocation to be the worshipper the Father seeks. Let it speak to you, and as it speaks, count the cost and pay the price. It will be worth it!

Christine Larkin
Senior Leader, Restoration House Churches
Author, Speaker, Prophetic Minister

INTRODUCTION

A few years ago, we found ourselves on an unexpected journey. Coming out of a challenging period, we entered into a whole new world of discovery about the importance of night and day worship and prayer. Our lives look radically different now from what we might have anticipated. We are convinced that we have stumbled upon truths which will change individual lives, communities and nations, and prepare the way for the return of King Jesus.

Our hearts are full of gratitude to our heavenly Father; we are more convinced than ever of His absolute faithfulness and extravagant love towards us.

We are also very grateful to our family and friends who have walked with us, believed in us, prayed for us and cheered us on as we have explored fresh horizons. This book is a response to the encouragement of many of you to:

Write the vision;
make it plain on tablets,
so he may run who reads it.
Habakkuk 2:2

We hope we have managed it. We pray that the Holy Spirit will speak to you as you read; that He will illuminate specific things He wants you to catch and give you wisdom about how to implement what He is showing you.

Robin and Claire Dillamore
July 2019

CHAPTER 1

ALL ABOUT DESIRE

'One thing have I desired'
Psalm 27:4 (KJV)

For You to die was all about desire
And that desire was me.

It was 6am on Saturday morning at David's Tent 2018.[i] Sixteen hours down, fifty-six to go. Our friend Jonny Riggs was leading worship and, although I (Robin) had a prayer meeting at 6.30am, I wanted to catch some of Jonny's set first.

> *For You to die was all about desire*
> *And that desire was me.*

As we repeated these lines, I had a cascade of revelation.

Until you experience it, it is hard to describe how much understanding can flood through your heart and mind as you are caught up in worshipping Jesus. Many of you reading this will know exactly what I mean! As we sang the words over and over, at one level my mind was thinking, 'Does this even make sense?' Yet at the same time my heart was flooded with a myriad of thoughts: *Wow, Jesus, You didn't die because You had to; You wanted us so much that You did it willingly! . . . I just want to be with You; that's all I want; that's all that matters! . . . Lord, You're amazing; life with You is awesome . . . These wild worshippers here in a tent are understanding mysteries that the finest minds in the world can't grasp. You really do save Your best secrets for Your lovers!*

In two hours' time, we were due to have our daily forty-five minute meeting with the Team Builders, the four hundred and fifty amazing lovers of Jesus who are key to the success of David's Tent. I had woken up earlier feeling a Holy Spirit stirring to share with them all about King David and his tabernacle, the high point in history which gave the event its name. In that moment of worship, I knew what I needed to say – 'It's all about desire.'

What I said to the Team Builders that morning was something like this:

David's Tabernacle

David did not set up his tabernacle because he had to. Unlike Moses, he did not get a list of detailed instructions from God. It was all about desire! He just wanted to be as close to God as possible, and worship Him day and night. And he knew that God wanted this too. More than anything else, God wants to be close to His people.

This is why David was called a man after God's heart – he loved God so much that his desires were in tune with God's desires. The Lord did not have to tell him what to do, He simply put His desire in David's heart. And so the tabernacle of David was birthed – a glorious thirty-three year 'blip' in the Old Testament drama, which changed the course of history forever, and which holds powerful keys for us to rediscover.

David stumbled upon secrets that will transform the world. He did not go looking for them; he found them by accident, while sitting with a flock of sheep on the hills of Bethlehem. He fell in love with the Maker of the Universe, and discovered that God is looking for lovers. More than anything else, God wants to find people who desire intimacy with Him as their deepest longing. And He saves His best secrets for His lovers.

In His wisdom, God has given His strategy for 'world dominion' to a bunch of 'fools'. It is so simple that only lovesick worshippers will take it seriously. Worship is going to transform the planet! Nothing else will do it. Not half-hearted singing or empty repetition. Hearts that are ablaze with love; people who have discovered why they are on the planet – to pour out their lives in adoration at the feet of King Jesus.

Before you write us off as crazy, we invite you to consider the evidence. That's what this book is about. It is one of the best kept secrets of the Bible – the story of David's tabernacle and how it changed history. It is the reason the book of Psalms exploded into existence. It is why a mountain called Zion is the focus of so many prophetic scriptures. It reveals the power of day-and-night worship to transform nations. It is hidden in a bunch of verses scattered around the Old Testament. But when you piece these verses together, a picture comes together of staggering beauty and significance.

We are going to dive into King David's story very soon. But first we want to share with you a little of our own adventure, and how we chanced upon the truths we are so excited to tell you about.

Notes

i. David's Tent is an annual three-day worship festival in West Sussex which began in 2012. The worship continues non-stop for 72 hours, and the event is currently attended by about 5,000 worshippers each year.

CHAPTER 2

DAVID'S TENT –
WHERE IT ALL BEGAN

'Something shifts when we decide to make the
first priority loving Him . . . He can't resist coming
to us when we make a space for Him.'[i]
Tiffany Buhler

Claire's Story

It was the summer of 2013 and I was completely worn out.
The previous eighteen months had been a crazy whirlwind
of change and transition and it had taken its toll.

2012 had been great it many ways; it had seen the
thrill of my promotion to a senior leadership role in the
secondary school where I taught, and the very happy
wedding of one of our daughters. There was much to
celebrate! But I struggled to adjust when all three of our
adult children left home within weeks of each other, and
there were aspects of my new job and Robin's business
which were very demanding. We were also part of the
leadership team of a local church which was experiencing
significant difficulties. We spent hours talking, praying
and seeking to resolve issues which only got worse, whilst
trying to keep the show on the road with the everyday life
of the church.

The end result was that my health began to suffer, and
our marriage was also feeling the strain. My tendency to

process stress externally (and loudly sometimes!) meant that Robin (who is a 'words of affirmation' guy) was getting hurt practically every time I opened my mouth.

It should have been a relief when one of our fellow leaders suggested that I take a sabbatical. I had been screaming out to God for weeks that I just wanted to stop and get off this merry-go-round, but my initial reaction was fear. I simply could not cope with the thought of stepping out of church leadership if Robin stayed on, because I thought it would increase the disconnection between us. I sat hugging my knees in a bean bag in the corner of our living room, conflicted beyond belief, trying not to sob, crying out silently for God to do something. Then I heard Robin say, 'If Claire's going on sabbatical then I am too. I'm doing it with her.' Up until that point I don't think I had ever loved him more. Relief flooded my soul. Although I knew it would be a long haul, I think I knew then that everything was going to be OK.

So in June 2013 we began an open-ended sabbatical. We had no idea for how long the Lord wanted us to draw aside, or whether we would ever be in church leadership again, but we did not care. Getting right with the Lord and each other, and resting and becoming healthy, were all that mattered. We had already booked a summer holiday in the south of France. After twenty-five years of marriage, it would be our first two whole weeks of unbroken time together, and the timing was perfect. It turned out to be Holy Spirit 'boot camp' in glorious sunshine, amid vineyards and olive groves, where we were able to hole up and start dealing with our stuff. The Lord was very gracious to us. We would have a day or two of fun and then it was as if He'd say, 'Let's look at this . . .' and help us to work through one issue at a time. He is indeed the Wonderful

Counsellor! It was both tough and glorious. After lots of tears and some heated conversations we returned home with a new togetherness, confident that God was calling us to an adventure-filled future, even though we had no clue what it would look like.

Enter David's Tent

There are times when Facebook comes into its own, and this was one of them. That August, I was online when a post from Jason Upton popped up.[ii] He said he was looking forward to being in the UK soon. Jason Upton in the UK? Oh my! I clicked on the link, thinking I would be happy to drive miles for this event, to find that he was going to be leading worship at David's Tent in West Sussex at the end of the month. I checked the dates and immediately hit a problem: Robin had work commitments and could not go. I was not sure what to do; the new togetherness we were experiencing felt fragile and in need of protection. Would it be OK for me to go alone and risk damaging what the Lord was doing with us? After some prayer and discussion, we felt peaceful about it, so I booked with two weeks to go and headed off down south with a good friend on an epic road trip which would change our lives.

I was only there for forty-eight of the seventy-two hours but that was enough. I will never forget the big smiles and warm welcome we received when we arrived at the site, making me feel immediately safe and at ease, nor the intensity of walking into a wall of worship as I entered the big blue tent for the first time. There were two thousand delegates that year and every single person seemed fully engaged with ministering to the Lord. Some were singing, some dancing, some waving flags, some kneeling or lying prostrate, but all focused on Jesus, pouring out their hearts to Him. I felt welcome but like I did not fit. 'This used to be me,' I thought. I had been a worshipper since I met Jesus as a child, but at that moment it felt like a previous life, and I did not know what to do. At the same time, I was impacted by a mix of delight and frustration. 'I *knew* this was possible,' I said to myself, 'I *knew* it was possible to just worship for hours, and go where the Holy Spirit leads without interruption.' I felt like I had stumbled upon treasure I had always believed existed, but had never made the time to search out or explore.

Other than the train wreck of thoughts and emotions in my mind, I did not feel anything. Sometimes going through the motions is OK. I learned as a teacher that if you use assertive body language in a classroom, your emotions often catch up. I love what worship leader Steffany Gretzinger says about singing the lyric 'You are good!': 'You can either sing it *because* you believe it, or *until* you believe it.' This was definitely a case of 'until', so I did the only thing I could think of, and started to copy what everyone else was doing. It did not feel fake; rather it felt like relearning a skill I had lost. It was not long before I began to feel the Lord's presence and remembered how to worship – like jumping into a pool again when you haven't been swimming since last summer.

Encounters in Worship

Worship is one of the most vulnerable things we can do. When we open our hearts fully to the Lord, and start to let go, we take the risk of exposing everything inside us, and 'stuff' comes to the surface. I had so much 'stuff' in there, it did not take long for that to happen! That's when it is easy to get stuck. You are in the Lord's presence, delighting in Him, and then suddenly you are experiencing anger or hurt all over again as emotions rise up within you. I am so grateful for the wisdom and insight of the leaders at David's Tent. Their experience told them this would happen for many people. So they ensured that a skilled ministry team was available, and that frequent encouragement was given to 'ask someone to pray for you if things come up, *with the goal of dealing with it quickly, so that you can get back into His presence again.*' Two or three times I accessed this wise and gentle help and felt issues which had been stuck to me for months simply leave. On one occasion, I blurted out to a lovely lady, 'I've been dealing with a pile of rubbish for months.' She simply smiled and laid hands on me and waited. As she did, Jesus showed me a vision of Himself dressed in white and carrying a shovel. He literally removed a pile of horse manure from around me, without becoming the slightest bit dirty Himself. There was no judgement, criticism or unsolicited advice from anyone, just love and acceptance.

The Harp in My Heart

My biggest breakthrough came sovereignly through a prophetic experience. I saw Jesus come and stand in front of me and reach into my heart to draw out an object, which He then presented to me. I held out both hands to receive it but I could not see what it was because it was wrapped in a white cloth. I knew immediately it was not simply a covering but a burial shroud; the thing He had pulled out of my heart and given to me was dead.

As I began to feel around the object through the cloth, the Lord spoke to me telling me to unwrap it. It is fair to say I was not keen! I did not particularly want to see what the dead thing looked like, but I was comforted by the fact that it had hard edges and did not seem to be a body or a skeleton. The shroud came off cleanly and easily and I found myself holding a beautiful little harp. My first thought was 'How did that get there?' followed quickly by, 'What is it? What does it mean?' I honestly had no idea. 'It's worship,' the Lord said. 'The worship in your heart has been stifled and has died. I'm giving it back to you alive, releasing fresh songs and fresh sounds, setting your heart and voice free to soar again. The liberty in you will set others free.'

I understood immediately what He meant. I had not completely stopped worshipping, but the fire, the life and the joy I had once known had left me. The outward expression of my inward life had died – the call to sing prophetically, to release and write new songs, and to lead others into a deeper experience of His presence. I think I had even forgotten it was in my heart. It was so good to know that He was giving it back to me! It felt like part of who I was had been missing and was coming back to life, making me whole. In the months that followed, reading the Psalms in The Passion Translation, I discovered that the 'harp in my heart' is a biblical concept.[iii] But at that moment, it was just me, Jesus and a glorious resurrection!

Space in His Presence – the Place of Encounter

I was so grateful, and realised that what had made this encounter possible was simply *space in His presence*. The atmosphere and ethos at David's Tent, and the focus on ministering to Jesus in worship without interruption, had created space for me to encounter Him, and experience freedom that I do not think would have happened in months of counselling. Something in me began to rise up. If this could happen for me, how many other people was it happening for? If this could happen in a tent in West Sussex, then why not in a living room, or a church building in Chester, or anywhere else for that matter? If we could create space in His presence by simply worshipping for hours, then how many other people could encounter Him in the ways they needed?

Togetherness

Another highlight of David's Tent that year was when Melissa Helser gave her testimony. Melissa, and her husband Jonathan David, have been worship leaders at David's Tent every year since it began.[iv] Unusually, in the middle of their worship set, Melissa took the microphone and spoke powerfully from her testimony of living with a chronic illness, releasing an urgent prophetic word over the UK about breaking the power of disappointment using the antidote of thanksgiving. At the same time as receiving her word for my nation and my own life, I was deeply impacted by what I saw of Melissa and Jonathan's relationship on stage; their togetherness in ministry was palpable. I started crying out to God again – 'Lord, what You've done in me this weekend, *please* do it in Robin too! Please let him not miss out from not having been here! Please let me not have to explain what You've done in me. Let it just be seen!' As I prayed, it was as if Jonathan faded out from the stage, and Robin stood there in his place, leading worship and playing the guitar. That took me by surprise! 'It would be great if that happened,' I thought, 'the two of us leading worship together.'

I returned home so free it did not seem possible. The colours were brighter, the air sweeter and my heart was singing again for the first time in months. I was not anxious about how Robin and I would reconnect when I got there. I was more interested to see what the Lord would do, and I suppose a little nervous about making sure I held onto all God had done in me. What I encountered when I arrived was incredible.

Robin's Story

I had been on my own worship journey in the run-up to David's Tent 2013. Looking back, I can see how the Spirit was stirring up yearnings in my heart that had been buried deep inside for a long time.

In the spring of that year, we had a house guest for a few weeks. She loved to worship and would regularly go to her room to play her guitar and sing. This both inspired and challenged me. One week, she came along with me to a home group meeting I was leading. While we drank coffee at the beginning, she picked up a guitar that was lying there and started playing. We ended up spending the whole evening worshipping. Every so often she looked over at me as if to say, 'Do you want to do something else now?' But we all just wanted to carry on. It was the best home group meeting ever!

Around this time, Bill Johnson's book *Hosting the Presence* made a deep impact on me. Holy Spirit was helping me connect with my heart's desire to live as a 24-7 worshipper. One thing Bill wrote particularly struck me. In the Old Testament, he said, the people of God used to pitch their tents around the Tabernacle containing the Ark of the Covenant: 'Israel camped around the Presence of

God, while the church often camps around a sermon.' This was so liberating! For years, I had bought the lie about worship being insignificant; that it is just something we do to prepare our hearts for 'the preach'. But the truth was exploding inside me. The realisation was dawning that worship is so much more than that. It is not the 'warm-up', it is the main thing. When I worship God, my heart comes fully alive.

I was starting to break out of the prisons in my thinking and, like Paul and Silas, I was singing my way to freedom! I was asked to speak at a church holiday in France that spring. It was an enjoyable few days, but some of the most memorable moments of the trip for me were the two twelve-hour car journeys. I played worship albums and sang along loudly all the way, both there and back. I do not know how my two passengers felt about this, but I was finding my voice! There was a passion inside of me that was bursting to come out.

God also got my attention through prophetic words and encouragement. One Sunday morning, a good friend sat between Claire and me at a church meeting. She was unusually impacted by the experience of hearing us singing on either side of her. Over the following weeks, she told us repeatedly that there is something special about our combined sound. Up until then, we had never led worship together, just the two of us. Another friend, who knew nothing about what was going on inside me, prophesied that we were songbirds, with one voice coming out of our togetherness, calling the church to awaken.

While Claire was at David's Tent that August, God graciously met with me too. Although I could not be with Claire at the event, I was hungry for more of God. So I decided to spend time with Him in our living room, worshipping to the accompaniment of Bethel Music worship videos. I experienced a beautiful sense of God's Presence and His goodness. He spoke in my heart about Claire and me leading worship together, so I decided to start learning the guitar. This was something I had briefly tried almost thirty years before, but quickly given up on. When Claire came home, I was amazed to discover that she had had a vision of us leading worship together.

And so we journeyed on together from there; and we do lead worship together now. It certainly hasn't all been plain sailing, but we are enjoying the ride! Our story continues in the next chapter.

Notes
i. Tiffany Buhler in Sean Feucht & David Fritch, *Burn 24-7 – A Collision of Vertical Worship and the Great Commission* (Burn 24-7, 2014), ch. 2
ii. Jason Upton is a prophetic worship leader whose ministry we love (https://jasonupton.com).
iii. See, for example, Psalm 43:4 TPT.
iv. https://www.jonathanhelser.com

CHAPTER 3

JOURNEYING ON

'The pursuit of the presence of God has been,
without exception or exaggeration,
the prevailing passion and the common
purpose of all the saints in every
generation since the time of Christ.'[i]

Pete Greig

If we can create space in God's presence by worshipping for hours, then people will encounter Him. This simple conviction took root in our hearts and resulted in a sense of responsibility to do something about what we believed. There was nothing to stop us! We did not yet know anything about other worship movements like Burn 24-7, we just knew we had a living room and some musical instruments and we had to do something. And so we started, in fits and spurts at first. We invited people to our home who loved to worship, and experimented with evenings of worship with no designated leader. It was hard to explain what we had seen, and what we were going after, but we persevered, even though it was sometimes messy.

Jumping Off a Cliff

As 2014 drew to an end, I (Claire) had begun the new academic year and felt like I was 'wading through treacle'. This was not like me – I had a dream job (even though it was stressful) and I usually love fresh starts, especially the beginning of a new term. As I processed how I felt, I became increasingly unsettled. Robin had begun to reduce his hours at work to free up more time for the Lord, and I wanted to do the same. We had felt a call to ministry together since before we were married, but so many things had got in the way over the years. We had started to wonder if the fulfilment would have to wait until we retired.

During that season, not knowing what I was pondering, a good friend told us about how the Lord had called her to give up her job and launch into ministry, with no safety net. I had been deeply challenged: 'I wish I could do that, but I can't,' I thought. There followed several weeks of talking with the Lord and praying through the issues which held me back from that kind of decision – mostly fear of what people would think, it turned out, and not at all to do with finance!

It soon became clear that my time in education was at an end; God was inviting me to take a deep breath, jump off a cliff and hand my notice in. I was totally relieved and freaked out all at the same time! We had no idea exactly what the space we were creating was for, but we were confident that the Lord would make it clear as we walked with Him. I made an appointment to see my headteacher and explained to her that I felt it was time to move on. Her first question to me was, 'Are you going to train for the ministry?' 'Not exactly!' I replied. I was moved to hear that she did not want to lose me, and grateful that she nevertheless offered her full support.

Birth of a House of Prayer

On the church front, our sabbatical had come to a natural end that year, and we had been encouraged back into leadership. The challenges the church had been experiencing had proved intractable and so we made the difficult decision as a leadership team to bring things to an end. We were left with a church building that we no longer needed, and so we decided to sell it so that we could draw a line and move on. Early in 2015, we were delighted to receive an offer from a property developer for the site, but the process did not go smoothly. It is sometimes difficult, isn't it, to tell whether glitches are from the Lord, because He wants us to stop, or from the enemy and need powering through? It is encouraging that there are biblical examples of people working through similar issues.

Robin was at a conference with a wise prophetic friend and mentioned the situation to her. She asked an interesting question: 'Have you asked the Lord what His original intention was for the building?' It had not occurred to us to ask such a question. I remember vividly the phone call that evening. It was another pivotal moment. I was at home when Robin called. As he relayed the question to me, in my heart I turned it to the Lord and was immediately taken into a vision. I was in the church building, in the smaller of two halls which had been used for our youth and children's ministry. At the time, it was untidy and neglected, full of old furniture and broken toys. In the vision, it was cleaned out and redecorated, warm and inviting, full of fire and glory and crammed with people worshipping.[ii] Over my shoulder, I could see the larger hall behind me, and there were people from the local community coming in and out, finding a safe place, chatting and drinking tea, whilst the worship was going on. I started yelling down the phone to Robin, 'I know what it is! I know what we need to do!'

It was a collision of our dream to have a place of unhindered worship, and the Lord trusting us with the stewardship of premises where this could become a reality. He was inviting us into a place where we could put into practice what we believed.

Prophetic Encouragement

Things rarely work out exactly as you plan them. In our heads, I was going to finish work in July, get some rest over the summer and then spend the autumn sorting out the worship room. Robin was going to continue to reduce his hours at work. It was all going to be wonderful.

Then, two weeks into the summer holidays, my dad died. (It was not entirely unexpected as he was eighty-eight and in poor health.) We spent a whole week before he passed sitting vigil at his bedside with my family, and then a fortnight sorting out funeral arrangements with my mum, who was herself very frail. By the end of the summer we were both tired and ready for a break. We were therefore glad that we had taken advantage of Claire's first September out of teaching and arranged to go to South Carolina for MorningStar's annual HarvestFest conference. It proved to be another life-changing trip.

We knew almost no one at the conference, and therefore spoke to many new people. On every occasion, we were asked, 'So what do you guys do?' The only response we could find was to talk about our vision for our prayer room. We were met with a torrent of encouragement from enthusiastic and friendly Americans, along the lines of, 'That is awesome!' and 'You should totally do that thing!' It was just what we needed to hear, and we began to believe that we might actually be able to do it!

MorningStar is a highly prophetic environment, and we benefited from much genuine prophetic ministry during that week. On one occasion we found ourselves in a fundraising event for their own 24-7 house of prayer (the Bob Jones Vision Center). We had not intended to be there; we just wandered in through an open door because we saw a friend. A lovely guy called Gene, who knew nothing about us, came over and offered to prophesy over us. By the Spirit, he described our vision to a tee, affirming it was the calling of the Lord. By then we were convinced, but there was still an unspoken question in our hearts: 'Lord, we think this is supposed to be 24-7, but we do not want to presume. That feels really big.' As Gene turned to walk away, he looked over his shoulder and said, 'And by the way, it's 24-7.' That settled it.

When we returned home, instead of going back to school, I rolled up my sleeves and began cleaning out the place that is now our worship room. It took several weeks, but it was wonderful to see the vision begin to take shape. We started to hold informal meetings in the space and experiment with unstructured times of worship with small groups of friends. We began living the dream!

The Slow Burn

By February 2016 the room was ready for visitors and we invited Godfrey Birtill to come and lead the first of our monthly 'Heart to Heart' worship nights.[iii] We were excited, and a little relieved, that people came. We were willing to turn up and worship even if it was only the two of us, but we were also eager for others to experience the Lord's presence, and learn to minister to Him as their First Love.

Almost every month since then we have met on a Friday night to worship. We started with worshipping for ninety minutes in two forty-five minute 'sets'. That felt like a huge stretch to begin with but we persevered. It took over a year for the ninety minutes to feel 'normal' and then we felt the Lord challenge us to go for three hours. Three years later we are worshipping for between five and six hours with the occasional extended event every few months (as we write we are planning for a hundred hours in June 2019). This gentle 'on ramp' was deliberate – we do not intend to burn out again, and we believe from experience that capacity increases sustainably as we keep stretching just a little beyond our comfort zone.

As the development of our worship room continued, we discovered that we were not alone; others out there were on a similar journey of discovery. We became more involved with David's Tent, joining the volunteer team, and began to find out more about other worship and prayer movements such as Burn 24-7. One person in particular whose ministry and writings impacted us at this time was Sean Feucht, the founder of Burn 24-7. Sean and his wife Kate's story of sacrificial pursuit is compelling.[iv]

Hillside

Through these connections we heard about a residential worship school called Hillside Intensive, named for the time King David spent learning to worship as a boy, on the hillside above Bethlehem with his sheep. It seemed just what we needed – ten days set aside simply to worship and to continue our learning journey. We decided that Claire should go. (She had such a great time that Robin went the following year.)

In fact, I (Claire) nearly didn't go. Insecurity and fear nearly won. I nearly didn't apply; once accepted, nearly pulled out; and once there, nearly came home. *What if I* am the oldest there? I was. *What if the others can all sing and play really well?* They could. *What if they don't like me and think I'm a fraud?* We were all in the same boat – everyone else had their own insecurities to overcome. How delighted is our heavenly Father when we press through and trust Him with our hearts?

In one memorable session, one of Hillside's leaders, Allan Boehm, was pacing the floor preaching his heart out on 2 Kings 13 – the story of Elisha calling on King Joash to strike the ground with his arrows. Joash struck the ground three times, instead of five, six, seven or eight, and so stopped short of the complete victory he could have won. Allan's challenge to us was this: In the middle of mundaneness and trials, especially when we do not feel like it, what does our five, six, seven or eight look like? How are we going to 'press beyond'?

I could not contain myself. I didn't wait for Allan to finish speaking. I stood up and shouted out, 'I know what mine is! I have to get my butt to the prayer room!' I was inspired and deeply challenged. If what we had been learning was to become a reality, I actually had to shift and behave differently. Monthly worship nights were great but there was more. We had an underlying vision for 24-7 worship and prayer, and I could not just wait passively for it to happen, or expect someone else to do it. I needed to make a public confession. The rest of the session fell apart (in a good way) as others made their own declarations, and I felt on fire with a passion I have been seeking to fuel ever since.

When I returned home, I did begin to 'get my butt to the prayer room', and have continued to do so since. The memory of my experience at Hillside continues to provide impetus, especially when things get tough. Developing new habits takes time and effort. I love how Chris Burns describes it in his book *Pioneers of His Presence*:

> All of the heroes in the faith . . . have one common denominator: they were all lovers of God whose deepest desire was to know Him. They hungered for intimate relationship with Him . . . They laboured in the art of the secret life with God.[v]

Discovering Biblical Foundations

At Hillside, we were both inspired by the insights of different speakers into the biblical foundations of night and day worship and prayer. Our appetites were whetted. Hungry for more, we enrolled in Burn 24-7's online ministry school and were even more deeply impacted by a module on biblical foundations. We had no idea that the things we had been experiencing in worship had such an extensive biblical basis. It was paradigm-shifting stuff! We had been Christians for years and thought we had a reasonably sound grasp of the Bible, but this was all brand new.

We simply could not get enough and spent hours researching and discussing together what we were learning, becoming increasingly excited. Discovering the biblical basis for extended worship and prayer gave us a solid foundation. It gave us the *why* behind the *what* — principles we could use to communicate to others what we were doing. Principles are vital because practice (the *what*) is situation-specific, but principles (the *why*) are transferable. Others can't replicate our practice in their setting, but they can take hold of the same principles and use them as a framework. If the principles are sound, what works in one place will work in another. That's true of any kind of principle – in business or science, for example. But biblical principles are especially important because they derive from the heart of God and encapsulate eternal truths. We were thrilled to be developing language to communicate with others the principles which undergirded our vision.

Our biggest desire for this book is that it will equip you with biblical principles you can apply in your own setting, and language to communicate your vision to those around you. Our prayer is that all who read this will grasp what we did – that extended worship and prayer is part of God's masterplan for intimacy with His people, community transformation, unity and successful missional activity. We pray that revelation explodes on the inside of you, and propels you to seek Him for what He wants your specific response to be.

We invite you to join us on our journey of discovering the biblical foundations of extended worship and prayer.

Notes

i.   Pete Greig, *Dirty Glory: Go Where Your Best Prayers Take You* (Hodder and Stoughton, 2016), ch. 3

ii. It was indeed restored to its original purpose – before our church had bought the premises, it had been owned by a different church which used that room as a sanctuary.

iii. Godfrey Birtill is a British prophetic intercessory songwriter and worship leader.

iv. Sean Feucht & David Fritch, *Burn 24-7: A Collision of Vertical Worship and the Great Commission* (Burn 24-7, 2014), ch. 1

v.   Chris Burns, *Pioneers of His Presence* (Chris Burns, 2014), ch. 6

THE TENT ON THE MOUNTAIN

'David's tent was the only sanctuary ever
established on Mount Zion ... Zion is one
of the main symbols in Scripture ...
it foreshadowed the joyful heavenly
assembly to which we ascend in worship,
which in turn is a foretaste of the
assembly at the end of all things.' [i]

Peter Leithart

There is an uprising of worship and prayer happening around the globe.

Over the last twenty years, there has been a surge of prayer and worship initiatives. In the very same month (September 1999) that the International House of Prayer in Kansas City extended its prayer and worship to a full 24-7 schedule, the '24-7 Prayer' movement was founded by Pete Greig in Chichester, in the south of England. Is this a coincidence, or is God trying to get our attention?

It is not just in the USA or Europe either. 24-7 prayer spaces can now be found in every continent of the world. In the underground church in China, many of God's people have been feeling a burden to pray day and night. A network of Chinese churches has more than twenty different 24-7 houses of prayer; until they were visited by Christians from the West, these saints were totally unaware of similar movements taking place elsewhere.[ii]

The prophet Malachi spoke of a future day when prayer and worship would fill the earth:

> 'For from the rising of the sun to its setting My Name will be great among the nations, and in every place incense will be offered to My Name, and a pure offering. For My Name will be great among the nations', says the Lord of hosts.
>
> *Malachi 1:11*

From Revelation 5:8 we know that incense represents the prayers of the saints, so we see in this verse a prediction that worship and prayer to God will spread all around the globe.

Rebuilding David's Tabernacle

The prophet Amos foretells the rebuilding of David's tent:

> I will raise up the tabernacle of David, which has fallen down and repair its damages; I will raise up its ruins, and rebuild it as in the days of old.
>
> *Amos 9:11 (NKJV)*

It is fascinating that God promises to rebuild David's tabernacle, which was just a simple tent. We would have expected Him to be much more interested in rebuilding Solomon's temple, which was the most ornate and magnificent edifice imaginable. Surely, such a dwelling place would be far more suited to the King of the Universe?

Amos' prophecy was quoted by the apostle James at the Council of Jerusalem, a crucial moment in the development of the early church (Acts 15:16). There is a clue here, a hint that there's an important connection between what David did and God's purposes for the church today.

At one level, David's tent is a picture of the church. We are all 'being built together into a dwelling place for God by the Spirit' (Ephesians 2:22). And we are called to be a people, all over the earth, who are continually full to overflowing with God's Spirit, 'speaking to one another in psalms and hymns and spiritual songs, singing and making melody with [our hearts] to the Lord' (Ephesians 5:18-19 NASB).

But there is another aspect to the rebuilding of David's tabernacle. God was very specific in saying that the fallen tent *of David* would be rebuilt. And intriguingly, the prophecy in Amos goes on to predict a harvest of supernatural proportions:

'Behold, the days are coming,' declares the Lord,
'when the ploughman shall overtake the reaper
and the treader of grapes him who sows the seed;
the mountains shall drip with sweet wine,
and all the hills shall flow with it.'

Amos 9:13

The prophet is pointing to a connection between the restoration of David's tent and a mighty move of the Spirit, which many believe is the end-time harvest spoken of by Jesus (see Matthew 13:39).

The Significance of Zion

There are many references to Zion in the Psalms and prophetic scriptures. When the Bible refers to Zion, it is referring primarily to the period of David's reign in

Jerusalem. *For it was only during this time that the ark of the covenant (the seat of God's presence) was situated on Mount Zion, in David's tabernacle.*[iii] So Zion speaks of the tabernacle of David, which, as we shall see, was a place of continual worship.

Evidence of the importance of Zion for us can be found in the book of Hebrews. The writer tells us, in chapter 12, that *we* have come to Mount Zion:

> For you have not come to what may be touched . . .
> But *you have come to Mount Zion* and to the city of the living God, the heavenly Jerusalem, and to innumerable angels in festal gathering, and to the assembly of the firstborn who are enrolled in heaven, and to God, the judge of all, and to the spirits of the righteous made perfect, and to Jesus, the mediator of a new covenant, and to the sprinkled blood that speaks a better word than the blood of Abel.
>
> *Hebrews 12:18-24 (emphasis ours)*

God is saying that what happened in David's time, on Mount Zion, was a foretaste of something He wants us to experience today. There is a heavenly reality into which we can now enter.

In his simple tent, David did something which had never been done before. He established day and night worship and prayer, centred around the presence of God, with open access for all the people. What he did was not just an anomaly of history. It was an event of 'global, even cosmic significance.' [iv]

The history of David's tabernacle is a signpost to us of the importance of day and night worship and prayer. These are governmental activities, as we discover in Psalm 110. This Psalm is the one most quoted in the New Testament, and it says of Jesus,

> The Lord will stretch forth Your strong sceptre *from Zion*, saying, 'Rule in the midst of your enemies.'
>
> *Psalm 110:2 (NASB, emphasis ours)*

As we have seen, Zion was a place of day and night worship, where God was enthroned continually on the praises of His people. So the implication of this verse is that the rule of King Jesus will be powerfully displayed through a people who worship and praise Him day and night, just as the Israelites did on Mount Zion.

Prophetic Fulfilment

Could we be seeing the fulfilment of these prophecies in Malachi, Amos and the Psalms today? Could this be why, in the last two decades, there has been such an explosion of day and night worship and prayer all over the earth? Is the Lord rebuilding the fallen tabernacle of David, as He promised? We believe He is.

The tabernacle of David on Mount Zion was key to changing the whole nation. If it had kept going for longer, who knows what would have happened! David gave us a glimpse of what is possible now. What he did was of strategic significance. But that's not *why* he did it, as we will see in the next chapter.

Notes
i.   Peter J. Leithart, *From Silence to Song: The Davidic Liturgical Revolution* (Canon Press, 2003), Preface
ii. Billy Humphrey, *Unceasing: An Introduction to Night & Day Prayer* (Forerunner Publishing, 2009, 2015), ch. 1
iii. Before this period, from the days of Joshua (Josh 18:1) until the time of Eli (1 Samuel 1:3), the ark was in Shiloh. It was then captured by the Philistines before being returned to Israel seven months later (1 Samuel 6:1). The ark ended up in the town of Kiriath-jearim, where it remained throughout the days of Samuel and Saul, until David brought it to Zion (1 Samuel 7:2, 1 Chronicles 13:3-5). Then, within a few years after David's death, the ark was moved to Mount Moriah, the site of Solomon's temple (2 Chronicles 3:1).
iv. Tamara Eskenazi, quoted in Peter J. Leithart, *From Silence to Song: The Davidic Liturgical Revolution* (Canon Press, 2003), ch. 1

CHAPTER 5

A MAN AFTER GOD'S HEART

'The best workers will be the best lovers.' [i]
Chris Burns

We are living in exciting days. All over the earth, God is raising up people with hearts like David's – people who will lead the way in transforming the nations.

David's heart was the key to every success in his life. He was 'a man after God's heart' (Acts 13:22 and 1 Samuel 13:14). If we attempt to copy what he did, we won't succeed unless we have the same heart. It would be a mistake to try and imitate David's methods without having his heart.

The Heart God is Looking For

It is not hard to see why God loved David's heart. Over and over, the Bible describes the kind of people He's looking for:

> You shall love the Lord your God with all your heart and with all your soul and with all your might.
>
> *Deuteronomy 6:5*

> For the eyes of the Lord run to and fro throughout the whole earth, to give strong support to those whose heart is blameless towards Him.
>
> *2 Chronicles 16:9*

The people who know their God shall stand firm and take action.

Daniel 11:32

He has told you, O man, what is good; and what does the Lord require of you but to do justice, and to love kindness, and to walk humbly with your God.

Micah 6:8

Such verses – and there are many more like them – tell us that God is yearning for intimacy with His people. More than anything, He is searching for people who want to know Him, to walk with Him; people who will trust Him with their whole heart. In David, the Lord found such a man.

The Heart of David

The Psalms of David tell us a lot about his heart.[ii] They give us a 'sneak peek' into what intimacy looks like.

There was nothing hidden from God in David's life. Every emotion he experienced he turned to God in intercession or worship. In every season of his life, David walked with God. This is why Psalm 23 is so powerful and has become so well-loved. It has the ring of authenticity! In just six verses, this beautiful song contains the distilled wisdom of a man who experienced God's goodness and faithfulness in every high and low circumstance.

David came to know God, and fell in love with Him, long before he was famous. His love affair with his Creator was kindled in times of hiddenness and obscurity, as a lone shepherd boy on the hillside. For him, intimacy with God was not a means to an end. He had no plans to become king or transform a nation. He simply discovered the Friend of all friends, the One worthy of all his love, attention and devotion. And he decided to love Him with all his heart, soul and might, for all his days.

> One thing have I asked of the Lord,
> that will I seek after:
> that I may dwell in the house of the Lord
> all the days of my life,
> to gaze upon the beauty of the Lord
> and to enquire in His temple.
>
> *Psalm 27:4*

This verse, penned by David, reveals that David wanted to be a priest more than to be king! The emphasis here is 'that *I* may dwell', rather than 'that I may *dwell*.' He coveted the intimacy and closeness reserved for the Levitical priesthood, although he came from the tribe of Judah. And he yearned to dwell in the house of the Lord, like a priest, even when he had the comfortable lifestyle of a king with a palace.

In fact, what David longed for was an intimacy that even the high priest did not experience. For not even the high priest was able 'to gaze upon the beauty of the Lord': When he entered the holy of holies once a year, on the Day of Atonement, the priest was not able to see the Lord, because there were clouds of incense obscuring his view. David had glimpsed a different, superior kind of priesthood, one which was 'after the order of Melchizedek', and which would ultimately be fulfilled by Jesus (see Psalm 110:4 and Hebrews 6:20).

Psalm 27:4 perfectly summarises David's deepest longing, for fellowship with God. It is also a beautiful reflection of God's desire for intimacy with us. Look how closely David's prayer is mirrored in the prayer of Jesus:

> Father, I desire that they also, whom You have given me, may be with Me where I am, to see My glory that You have given Me because You loved me before the foundation of the world.
>
> *John 17:24*

Just as David longed to dwell in God's house, Jesus yearns for us to be with Him where He is. He longs for us to see His glory, emulating David's greatest wish, to gaze upon His beauty. When we consider this, we begin to see what God saw in David's heart that was so special.

A Heart That Remains Steadfast

After his shepherd-boy days, David's life had numerous twists and turns. He killed Goliath, and became a national hero overnight. At first King Saul loved David. But then Saul became insanely jealous of him. There followed a protracted, painful period in which David was running for his life, punctuated by brief periods of respite when Saul realised the error of his ways.

In all these episodes, one thing stayed the same – David's unswerving devotion to God. He turned every trial and every triumph into a cry for help or a song of praise. And no matter what he faced, he found that God was right there with him. Even in the gravest danger, he knew God would rescue him:

> I call upon the Lord, who is worthy to be praised,
> and I am saved from my enemies.
>
> *Psalm 18:3*

Even though I walk through the valley of the shadow
of death, I will fear no evil, for you are with me.

Psalm 23:4

In the crucible of extreme situations, David deepened
his intimacy with God. And he never lost his childlike
confidence that God hears and answers us when we
pray. When he became king, he wanted to bring the
whole of Israel under the canopy of this same divine love
and protection:

He who dwells in the shelter of the Most High
will abide in the shadow of the Almighty . . .
He will cover you with His pinions,
And under His wings you may seek refuge.

Psalm 91:1-4 (NASB)

A Heart for God Looks Like Something

Over many years as a Christian, I (Robin) have often heard
people say that David was 'a man after God's heart'. But it
is only recently that I've come to see that there is more to
this phrase than I had appreciated.

A few years ago, if you had asked me what made
David special, I might have pointed to the way he
defeated Goliath, and his famous remark, 'For who is
this uncircumcised Philistine, that he should defy the
armies of the living God' (1 Samuel 17:26). Or I could have
mentioned the way David danced before the Lord with all
his might, and his memorable response to his wife Michal
when she despised him:

'I will make myself yet more contemptible than this, and I will be abased in your eyes. But by the female servants of whom you have spoken, by them I shall be held in honour.'

2 Samuel 6:22

These incidents certainly demonstrate David's heart of devotion to the Lord. And the Psalms he wrote, quoted earlier, also give us great insights into his beautiful, worshipping heart. But there is another aspect we have tended to overlook. David showed that he was a man after God's heart more clearly than ever by the changes he made after he became king.

David's Momentous Changes

So, what did David do after becoming king, to demonstrate his heart for God?

First of all, he brought the ark of the covenant to Jerusalem. This was one of the first things he did as king. He wanted the presence of God to be at the very heart of the nation, so the whole nation would experience the blessing of walking in God's ways.

Secondly, he put the ark in a simple tent. This was not like Moses' tabernacle, which had a veil between God and the people. David's tent had no veil, and this meant the people could draw near to the presence of God. Here we see David's heart for all God's people to experience intimacy with God. He wanted the whole nation to know God like he did. This is also prophetic of the new covenant, where the veil is removed in Christ (2 Corinthians 3:14-16), as was powerfully demonstrated when the veil in the temple was torn in two (Matthew 27:51).

And thirdly, David initiated a programme of day and night worship around God's presence. David understood that God is enthroned on the praises of His people. (See Psalm 22:3.) So, through 24-7 worship, God was continually exalted and it was evident to all that He was the true King over the nation.

Motivated by Desire

We will look at David's momentous changes further in the next chapter. But first, let's pause for a moment and revisit another fascinating aspect of his actions. It was not just the decisions David made that were so ground-breaking, but *the way he made them.*

When Moses constructed a tabernacle for God's presence, God gave him a detailed template and instructions to follow. In fact, every aspect of life in Israel was governed by in-depth laws, which God gave to Moses, recorded in Exodus, Leviticus, Numbers and Deuteronomy. But none of the changes that David implemented was mentioned in these detailed laws. There is no record to suggest that God had commanded David to do what he did. Indeed, before bringing the ark of the covenant to Jerusalem, David consulted with the leaders and all the people about whether it would be good to do so (see 1 Chronicles 13:1-4). It seems unlikely he would have done this if he had received clear instructions from God. David was not acting on orders; he was inspired by desire. These changes came from longings in David's own heart.

This is not to suggest that David was just 'doing his own thing'. Without doubt his vision was God-given; the prophet Samuel also seems to have been instrumental in shaping it. Even though Samuel died a long time before

David's tent was built, 1 Chronicles 9:22 states that 'David and Samuel the seer established [the gatekeepers] in their office of trust.' This implies that David and Samuel had talked together about the plans for the tabernacle many years before David became king.[iii]

God is Looking for Lovers

David had discovered a secret that only lovers of God can truly know – God's preferred way of leading us is to put His desires in our hearts.

Delight yourselves in the Lord;
And He will give you the desires of your heart.

Psalm 37:4 (NASB)

Somehow, David had stumbled upon a New Testament reality, centuries ahead of time. This is the power of a worshipping heart! What David experienced was prophesied by Jeremiah and fulfilled in the New Covenant:

I will put My law within them and on their heart I will write it.

Jeremiah 31:33 (NASB)

When God said He would write His law on our hearts, He did not mean we would know the ten commandments 'off by heart'. The heart is the seat of our passions and desires. God was promising that a day would come when we would love the things He loves, and hate what He hates. This is the abundant life promised by Jesus. And somehow David got a sneak preview.

If we look at the gospels, we can find many examples of this principle in action. People followed Jesus not from a sense of duty, but because they were captivated by Him and wanted to be with Him. Think about these people:

- The disciples, who left homes, families and livelihoods to follow Jesus

- The woman who touched the hem of Jesus' robe and was healed of persistent bleeding (Luke 8:43-48)

- Peter, when he said to Jesus, 'If that's really You, Lord, command me to come to You on the water' (Matthew 14:28)

- Mary of Bethany, who poured expensive perfume on Jesus' feet and wiped them with her hair (John 12:1-8)

Each of these – and many more – were motivated by passionate desires that welled up inside them. None of them acted from a sense of obligation.

In Psalm 34:8, David wrote, 'Taste and see that the Lord is good!' God loves to give us a taste of His goodness; then we will be drawn by a longing for more of Him.

Jesus taught His disciples to live this way. He did not give them lots of detailed instructions. He gave them the Holy Spirit and taught them to rely on intimacy with Him. We see the same principle at work as we read through the book of Acts. This is why the apostles could write about a decision they had made and say that 'it seemed good to the Holy Spirit and to us' (Acts 15:28). Of course, it is not a licence for us to do as we please, for 'even Christ did not please Himself' (Romans 15:3 NASB). But it is learning to live in such a way that our hearts are in tune with God's heart.

You could say that God is taking a big risk in choosing to lead us through our desires. Instructions in black and white are much less open to misinterpretation! God-given desires can feel an awful lot like our own self-focused desires. This is why Hebrews 5:14 tells us we need, by trial and error, to learn the difference between good and evil, i.e. between godly desires and selfish ones. But God clearly believes it is a risk worth taking. Let's not make the mistake of thinking all desires are bad or selfish. If we do, we will miss out on one of God's most precious ways of communicating with us. He is looking for lovers and friends, not just servants.

I believe this principle – learning to be led by Spirit-inspired desires – is a key reason why worship is so critical to God's end-time strategy. The more we worship, the more we delight ourselves in the Lord. And the more we delight in Him, the more we become people with whom He can share His most precious longings. Passionate lovers of God will do exploits that go way beyond anything that a duty-bound servant would ever attempt. Chris Burns sums it up well when he says, 'The best workers will be the best lovers.'

In the next chapter, we'll look in more detail at the changes David implemented.

Notes
i.   Chris Burns, *Pioneers of His Presence* (Chris Burns, 2014), ch. 5
ii. David wrote at least 75 Psalms. Out of 150 in the book of Psalms, 73 state 'of David' in the title, and a further two – Psalms 2 and 95 – are attributed to him by New Testament writers. See Acts 4:25 and Hebrews 4:7.
iii. For more on this, see Billy Humphrey, *Unceasing: An Introduction to Night & Day Prayer* (Forerunner Publishing, 2009, 2015), ch. 2

CHAPTER 6

ISRAEL'S GOLDEN ERA

'Why is worship the first and highest priority in
the Kingdom of God? Because, if God is not at
the centre, then it ceases to be the Kingdom of
God, but of man. Continual worship keeps our
hearts in alignment with His Kingship.' [i]

David Fritch

David reigned in Jerusalem for thirty-three years. Spiritually,
this was Israel's Golden Era.

As we saw in the last chapter, David made sweeping
changes when he became king. His heart's desire was for
the whole nation:

- to know the blessing of walking in God's ways – so
  he brought the ark of the covenant to be with him
  in his new capital city

- to experience intimacy with God, just as he had –
  so he put the ark in a simple tent with no veil to
  separate it from the people

- to know that God was their true King – so he set
  up a programme of day and night worship

Let's look at these three themes in more detail:

1 – Prioritising God's Presence

Bringing the Ark to Jerusalem

Before David was king, Saul ruled Israel for forty years, from a town called Gibeah. The difference between David and Saul is perfectly illustrated in their respective attitudes towards the ark of God's presence. During Saul's reign, the ark was less than ten miles away, in Kiriath-jearim, yet Saul neither visited the ark, nor made any attempt to move it (see 1 Chronicles 13:3). By contrast, as soon as the people crowned David king over Israel, he started making plans to bring the ark to Jerusalem.[ii] David's number one priority was to have the presence of God at the heart of the nation.

It was an inspired idea to bring the ark to Jerusalem! With the benefit of hindsight, it seems an obvious thing to do. But remember, David was only Israel's second king, and the single example he had to follow was Saul's, whose reign had been disastrous. So David had to work out for himself what being a good king should look like.

A Bump in the Road

The ark had a journey of about nine miles to make from Kiriath-jearim to Jerusalem. The first attempt did not go smoothly at all! The cart hit a bump in the road, and a man called Uzzah lost his life when he reached out and touched the holy wooden chest, in order to steady it (1 Chronicles 13:5-14). The mistake David made was to transport the ark on a cart pulled by oxen. This was the method the Philistines had used, several decades earlier, when they returned the ark to Israel (1 Samuel 6:1-16). But it was not how the Levites had been instructed to carry the ark. They were meant to carry it on their shoulders, signifying God's desire for His presence to be carried by His people (Exodus 25:12-14; Number 7:9).

While David figured out what to do, the ark remained at the house of Obed-Edom. This man was greatly blessed the whole time that the ark was with him (1 Chronicles 13:14). It would be fascinating to know what this blessing looked like, but we can only imagine. It must have been spectacular, though, because it only took a few weeks for David to hear the news of Obed-Edom's good fortune!

Following Uzzah's death, David did some research and found out how God intended the ark to be carried (1 Chronicles 15:2). It is a mark of his humility, and his relationship with God, that he was willing to learn from his mistake. Even though he had been humbled in the sight of the whole nation, he continued to trust God. He did not allow pride to deflect him from his objective. And the remarkable prosperity of Obed-Edom was a sign to him that he was on the right track, with his plan to bring the ark to Jerusalem. Three months later, the mission was successfully accomplished, and the ark was brought to Mount Zion.

David – Visionary and Innovator

David was a visionary, a pioneer, and he was willing to experiment. He trusted that his heart was right before God. During his years worshipping on the hillside, he had developed an intimacy with God which took him way beyond the limitations of the law. He was centuries ahead of his time in so many ways. Nevertheless, David was on a learning curve. He still made mistakes, including the fatal error which led to the untimely death of Uzzah. Having a heart after God did not make him infallible. The same is true for us.

It is so encouraging that, after the incident with Uzzah, David did not stop innovating and breaking new ground. He was able to move on from the painful experience without allowing it to undermine his confidence. This resilience came from his life of intimacy with God. This is why David could say:

Those who look to Him are radiant;
their faces are never covered with shame.

Psalm 34:5 (NIV)

When the ark was finally carried into Jerusalem, he did a number of things that were unprecedented:

- He pitched a new tent for the ark on Mount Zion, even though the tabernacle of Moses was just a few miles away in Gibeon.

- He took off his royal robes and dressed like a priest, wearing a linen ephod.

- He danced before the Lord with all his might.

Nothing like this had ever been seen before. How exciting it must have been for the people who got to observe and participate in this unfolding drama!

2 – Intimacy with God

No Veil

There was something unique about David's tent. *There was no veil in it.* In the tabernacle of Moses, a heavy veil separated the presence of God from the priests. Then once a year, on the Day of Atonement, the high priest would enter behind the veil with the blood of sacrifices. But in David's tent there was nothing to separate God from His priests or His people. What is most important to God's heart is intimacy with His people. He wants to dwell among us, and for us to abide in His presence (see John 15:1-11 and John 17:24, for example). This is what David's tabernacle was all about. David caught God's heart for intimacy with His people. There was no veil, because God doesn't want anything to come between Himself and us.

Whilst the ark of God's presence rested on Mount Zion, the tabernacle of Moses still existed, about ten miles away on Mount Gibeon. The Bible does not give us a detailed description of the tent that David erected. 1 Chronicles 15:1 simply tells us that David 'prepared a place for the ark of God and pitched a tent for it', and 1 Chronicles 16:1 adds that 'they brought in the ark of God and set it inside the tent that David had pitched for it'. But we *do* know that this was not the tent that Moses had constructed. We read a few verses later that the tabernacle of Moses was in Gibeon:

> And he left Zadok the priest and his brothers the priests before the tabernacle of the Lord in the high place that was at Gibeon.
>
> *1 Chronicles 16:39*

This is confirmed by 2 Chronicles 1:3-4, which tells us that the tent at Gibeon was the one 'which Moses the servant of the Lord had made in the wilderness'.

Animal sacrifices continued at Gibeon, even though the ark was not there. But David had glimpsed something of the New Testament reality, that it is a sacrifice of *praise* God really wants:

Through Him then, let us continually offer up *a sacrifice of praise* to God, that is the fruit of lips that give thanks to His name.

Hebrews 13:15 (NASB, emphasis ours)

And so, around the ark of the covenant on Mount Zion, there was no shedding of blood after its inauguration, only day and night sacrifices of worship and praise.

Scary and Glorious

Imagine what it must have been like to climb up Mount Zion, knowing that you were approaching the ark of the covenant, the very seat on which God was enthroned. The incident of Uzzah, who died instantly when he touched the ark, would have been fresh in people's memories. It would be surprising if they were not at least a little afraid. But it must have also been exhilarating. This is what they were created for – intimate fellowship with the Maker of heaven and earth. And now, for the first time in living memory, *anyone* could come and draw near to the presence of God. It was not just for the chosen few – the priests and Levites – it was for everyone. These were scary and glorious times!

Even David, the king, was acutely aware of the need to check himself out before he made the journey up that mountain:

Who may ascend into the hill of the Lord?
And who may stand in His holy place?
He who has clean hands and a pure heart,
Who has not lifted up his soul to falsehood
And has not sworn deceitfully.
He shall receive a blessing from the Lord

And righteousness from the God of his salvation.
This is the generation of those who seek Him,
Who seek Your face – even Jacob.

Psalm 24:3-6 (NASB)

Today, because of the blood of Jesus, we can draw near to the presence of God with boldness and confidence. It is an awesome and amazing privilege that we can join in with the worship of the heavenly hosts around the throne of God. As the book of Hebrews says:

You have not come to a mountain that can be touched
... you have come to Mount Zion.

Hebrews 12:18, 22 (NASB)

3 – Unceasing Worship

Day and Night on Zion

Perhaps the most phenomenal achievement of David's reign was to establish a programme of night and day worship on Mount Zion. It began with Asaph and Obed-Edom and their relatives:

So David left Asaph and his brothers there before the ark of the covenant of the Lord to minister regularly before the ark as each day required, and also Obed-Edom and his sixty-eight brothers, while Obed-Edom, the son of Jeduthun, and Hosah were to be gatekeepers.

1 Chronicles 16:37-38

Amazingly, this man Obed-Edom, who was assigned the privileged role of a gatekeeper, was not an Israelite.

1 Chronicles 13:13 tells us that he was a Gittite, which means he came from Gath and was therefore a Philistine. Under the law, he should not have been there. But David seemed to understand that the grace of God supersedes the law. We also see here a foreshadowing of the day when David's tabernacle would be rebuilt and the Gentiles would come (Acts 15:16-17).

This company of worshippers expanded with the passage of time. By the end of David's reign, it had become a vast army of 4,000 gatekeepers and 4,000 musicians, led by 288 skilled singers (see 1 Chronicles 23:5 and 25:7). In today's money, the payroll bill for a work force of this magnitude would be at least ten million pounds *per month!* [iii]

Aligning Earth with Heaven

One of the intriguing aspects of this unceasing worship is the way it was structured. As David Fritch points out, the organisation of the worship in David's tabernacle bore 'a striking resemblance to the throne room scene in Revelation 4'.[iv] It was as though David had glimpsed the heavenly scene and was seeking to replicate it on earth:

- The worship was led by four prophetic musicians – Asaph, Heman and Jeduthun, plus David himself – just as four living creatures, covered with eyes, led the worship in heaven (1 Chronicles 25:1; Revelation 4:8).

- In David's tent there were twenty-four worship teams, led by the 24 sons of Asaph, Jeduthun and Heman (1 Chronicles 25:1-31). And in the heavenly worship scene in Revelation, there are twenty-four elders worshipping around the throne (Revelation 4:9-11).

- A multitude of worshippers in David's tabernacle (several thousand as we have seen) mirrored the angelic worship company, made up of 'many angels, numbering myriads of myriads and thousands of thousands' (Revelation 5:11).

- The non-stop worship on Mount Zion was a visible demonstration of the heavenly worship which continues 'day and night' around God's throne:

Day and night they never cease to say, 'Holy, holy, holy, is the Lord God Almighty, who was and is and is to come!'

Revelation 4:8

David brought into being on earth something which already existed in the heavens. In so doing, he created a powerful alignment between earth and heaven.

Evidence for 24-7 Worship in David's Tabernacle

We cannot point to a verse stating explicitly that worship in David's tabernacle was 24-7, but we believe it *was*, for the following reasons:

- In 1 Chronicles 16:37, we read that David 'left Asaph and his relatives there before the ark of the covenant of the Lord to minister before the ark *continually*, as every day's work required' (NASB).

- The 24 teams, comprising thousands of singers and musicians, would have been an ample workforce to keep the worship going around the clock. 1 Chronicles 9:33 also tells us that these Levites were 'on duty day and night'.

- Psalm 134:1 confirms that the worship carried on into the night: 'Come, bless the Lord, all you servants of the Lord, who stand by night in the house of the Lord!'

- David's tabernacle superseded the tabernacle of Moses as the resting place for the ark of the covenant. In Moses' tabernacle, there was a flame that burned continually and was never allowed to go out (see Leviticus 6:13). We believe David would have wanted the worship to continue uninterrupted around the ark to replace this perpetual flame.

- As we have seen, there are a number of parallels between the worship in David's tabernacle and the worship in heaven. Since the heavenly worship continues around the clock, it would be fitting for the earthly counterpart to be 24-7 too.

A National Transformation

The alignment between earth and heaven, brought about by David's tabernacle, was one key to the transformation of the whole nation during his reign. Saul, who was king before David, made a royal mess of things. In his reign, Israel became backslidden, and got into all kinds of difficulties. Saul's reign finally came to an end when he lost a major battle with the Philistines, and was killed along with his sons (see 1 Samuel 31). But at the end of David's reign, war had ceased in Israel and the nation had peace on all its borders. The nation was blessed in every way imaginable, and the kingdom that David handed on to Solomon was the most prosperous in the whole of Israel's history.

David's success was because of another key component: *the first thing he did as king was to bring the ark of God's presence right to the very centre of the kingdom.* When we worship God, Psalm 22:3 says that He is enthroned on our praises. By establishing day and night worship, David was continually enthroning the Kingship of God over his own kingship. It was the complete opposite of Saul. Saul's kingship was all about 'me' – he wanted to look important. But David was saying, 'It is not about me. I am exalting God as King over this kingdom.'

The activity in David's tabernacle was all about agreement between heaven and earth. A thousand years before Jesus taught us to pray, 'Your kingdom come, your will be done, on earth as it is in heaven' (Matthew 6:10), David modelled what it looks like for earth to line up with heaven. In the centuries after the time of David, every time God's people had a resurgence of success, it was because they reintroduced Davidic worship and prayer. The book of 2 Chronicles highlights that all the righteous kings who came after David ensured that day and night worship was re-established around the ark of God's presence. For example, in the days of King Joash and Jehoiada the priest, we read that there was 'rejoicing and singing, *according to the order of David*' (2 Chronicles 23:18, emphasis ours).

In the next chapter, we explore in more detail the history of 24-7 worship and what it means for us today.

Notes

i. David Fritch, *Enthroned: Bringing God's Kingdom to Earth Through Unceasing Worship and Prayer* (David Fritch, 2017), ch. 7

ii. The tribe of Judah recognised David as king straight after Saul's death, but it took seven years for the rest of Israel to follow suit. I imagine that David spent this time dreaming and preparing for the day when he would reign over the whole nation. See 2 Samuel 2:1 to 5:5.

iii. Based on an average annual salary of £15,000, it would cost £10.36 million per month to employ 8,288 people full-time.

iv. David Fritch, ibid, ch. 4

CHAPTER 7

LIVING IN DAVID'S LEGACY

'Our mission is to fill the world with
unending adoration, extravagant praise,
and the knowledge of His beauty.
The nations are our promised inheritance
while His presence is our true reward.'[i]
Sean Feucht

Biblical Restoration Movements

King David's reign in Jerusalem was a season of unsurpassed glory and national transformation. His son Solomon inherited an incredible kingdom and was perfectly positioned to live in the fulness of David's legacy. He started well (see 2 Chronicles 8:14-15), but it is incredibly sad that he chose not to continue to recognise God as the one true King (see 1 Kings 11:1-8). Within a generation, the kingdom was divided and in disarray.

Biblical history after the reigns of David and Solomon is mostly very depressing. We see king after king plunge the nation into despair, conflict and misery as a result of their idolatry. But there are occasional flashes of hope. As we saw in the previous chapter, in the five hundred years following King David's reign, every king who re-established the Davidic order of 24-7 worship brought the nation back into a place of blessing and victory. Take a look at the reigns of kings and leaders like Jehoshaphat, Joash, Hezekiah, Josiah, and Zerubbabel. They all discovered the same truth – that prioritising God's presence at the heart of the nation led to peace and prosperity.

New Testament Reality

This lifestyle of night and day worship and prayer is not only an Old Testament phenomenon. It is right at the start of the New Testament church, too. How many sermons have you heard about the day of Pentecost, and how the disciples were all huddled together in the upper room, terrified and hiding, until the Holy Spirit fell on them? That is not actually what the Bible says. Look at this excerpt from the end of the book of Luke, describing Jesus' ascension:

> And behold, I am sending the promise of my Father upon you. But stay in the city until you are clothed with power from on high . . . While He blessed them, He parted from them and was carried up into heaven. And they worshipped Him, and *returned to Jerusalem with great joy, and were <u>continually</u> in the temple blessing God.*
>
> *Luke 24:49-53 (emphasis ours)*

The Greek word for continually, *diapantos*, means just that – continually, constantly, for all time. What other response to the risen, ascended Christ could there be? Night and day celebration, rejoicing, worship and praise from the overflow of grateful, astounded hearts seems perfectly appropriate!

As the next days and weeks unfolded it seems probable that this pattern continued. Jesus was alive! Reading the account of the outpouring of the Holy Spirit in Acts 2, it seems like it happened in a public place where there was space for thousands of people to hear what was going on and to gather. It could even have been in the temple courts. In any case, it was early morning – the 'third hour'. What were they doing all together like that first thing in the morning? Sleeping? Having breakfast? Or worshipping and praying?

By the end of Acts 2, several thousand believers were in and out of each other's homes and the temple, day after day, worshipping, eating and learning together. There is such a sense of life, hope and joy as you read the account, and no sense of people keeping an eye on time. The unfolding saga of Acts continues to give us intriguing glimpses into the early church's experience of continual worship and prayer, both corporately and individually:

- Acts 5 – Several apostles were imprisoned for performing signs and wonders. An angel of the Lord came during the night to release them and instructed them to go to the temple and preach. They responded, 'entered the temple **at daybreak** and began to teach'. It seems like there was a crowd there at daybreak. Had they been there all night?

- There are repeated references to individuals praying at the 'third', 'sixth', or 'ninth' hour; there was a daily rhythm to their prayer life which continued **throughout the day.**

- Acts 7 – in Stephen's discourse, just before he is martyred, he appeals to the nation's history, specifically mentioning their **heritage of continual worship and prayer** under the leadership of Moses,

Joshua, David and Solomon; it was evidently a huge part of the foundation of the community of which Stephen was a part.

- Acts 12 – Peter is imprisoned and is sleeping when an angel wakes him up and sets him free. In the **middle of the night**, Peter goes straight to Mary's house where many 'were gathered together and were praying' (v.12). What an epic all-night prayer gathering that must have been!

- It seems that night time prayer and worship were a normal part of Paul's, and others', devotional lives, wherever they were. Acts 16:9 and Acts 18:9 – the Lord speaks to Paul in visions **in the night**. They were visions, not dreams; the implication is that Paul was awake and praying. Acts 16:25 – imprisoned, Paul and Silas were 'praying and singing hymns' at '**about midnight**'. 2 Corinthians 6:5 (KJV) – Paul describes 'watchings' (**wakeful nights given to prayer**) as part of his commendation to the Corinthians.

Revival History

24-7 worship and prayer has continued in the life of the church ever since. It is not a new idea. In our pursuit of the Lord's presence, we walk in the footsteps of countless believers who have discovered the value of putting continual worship and prayer at the heart of their corporate and individual lifestyles. Across the sweep of history, the third-century Desert Fathers, monastic communities of all persuasions, 17th-century mystics and contemplatives like

Jeanne Guyon and Brother Lawrence, and 18th-century pioneers like Charles Wesley and Count von Zinzendorf and his Moravian community have ploughed the ground fearlessly and shown us the way.[ii]

We can be grateful to contemporary pioneers whose names we may know – Mahesh and Bonnie Chavda, Mike Bickle, Pete Greig, and Sean Feucht, for example – for responding to the call of Jesus, seeking intimacy with Him in the secret place and establishing places of night and day worship and prayer in the nations. Perhaps we can be even more grateful to countless others whose names we may not know, but whose stories we encounter along the way, because we can recognise ourselves in them. They are ordinary and unseen, not seeking fame or glory, but only the presence of the Lord. We truly walk in the footsteps of giants, cheered on by the great cloud of witnesses, those who have gone before (Hebrews 12:1). It really doesn't matter *how* we pray or worship; what matters is *that* we pray and worship – 'at all times on all occasions' (Ephesians 6:18 MSG). We have nothing to lose and everything to gain!

Our Continuing Experiment

So this is what we are exploring right now. We are involved in a great and continuing experiment. We cannot unsee what we have seen and we are ruined for anything else. It certainly isn't plain sailing and we still have more questions than answers. But we are learning to live with uncertainty and to hold it in tension with an increasingly clear vision.

Right at the beginning of this crazy adventure we had the conviction, simply stated: 'If we worship more, stuff will happen in our city.' We thought we'd try it and see and, so far, we are encouraged to keep going. Our 24-7 'Presence House of Prayer' dream often seems a long way off, but we are inching towards it an hour at a time. We are writing this book at the beginning of our adventure. We honestly did not expect to see any fruit for at least ten years, and so we have been incredibly blessed that the Lord has allowed us to see things happen sooner than that. People from across denominations and streams in our city are coming together to worship and pray, and building strong friendships as they do. Young people from our neighbourhood have come into our worship meetings and given their lives to Jesus. People are sharing testimonies with us of personal and life-changing encounters with God in the prayer room, and we have witnessed some physical healings. People engaged with evangelism in the city have commented how much 'easier' the atmosphere is, when they are out on the streets the day after a time of extended worship. We believe this is just the start!

Begin to Dream

Years ago, when I was a teacher with a young family, I used to try and take a 'God day' every half term or holiday. I'd hope for my three children's holiday activities to coincide and I'd take off for the day in my car with the Lord, just driving wherever I felt the Holy Spirit telling me to go, worshipping and praying as I went. I remember vividly occasions when my heart was simply aching to find a place to stop and lie prostrate before the Lord, or somewhere I might find others worshipping and I could join in. I'd drive around small towns and villages in North Wales looking at every chapel I passed (testimonies to the 1904 revival), hoping somewhere might be open and someone might be worshipping, but I never found anywhere. Somewhere deep down inside my heart broke, and this dream began – to provide a space where anyone could go at any time to seek Him. I know He is all around, and we can find Him anywhere, but sometimes, designated consecrated spaces are really what we need.

Not everyone is called to spend hours in the prayer room, and not every church is called to host a prayer room. For some reading this, your response will be very personal and private. Some will be called to support in practical or financial ways, by providing physical space for people to meet, or by praying for and encouraging those who are at the 'coal face'. But imagine what our towns and cities would look like if there were an expression of night and day worship and prayer in every one of them! Imagine how it would feel to live in a place where you knew someone was exalting Jesus continually, and praying for the community and its people! Imagine if there was a physical place in your neighbourhood where you could go any time you needed, away from distractions, simply to seek Him, worship, pray and pursue His presence!

Missionaries at Home

Over the course of 2017, getting to the prayer room regularly became an increasing challenge, even though we lived only a couple of miles away. We persevered, but began to feel the pull of the Lord to relocate so we could be on the doorstep, and realise our dream of living in community at the same time. The Lord spoke to us out of 1 Chronicles

9:26-27 about the 'chief gatekeepers' lodging around the house of the Lord and 'opening it for prayer every morning'. We were also encouraged by the testimony of some missionary friends whose ministry was based around a weekly rhythm of worship and prayer, prioritised above ministry opportunities. Their experience was that doors opened to them, and that the circumstances around them changed as they committed to seeking the Lord together and worshipping extravagantly to enthrone Him in their community. As we listened to them, the Lord spoke to us about identifying ourselves as missionaries to the council estate where our worship centre is situated. Our intention is to establish a House of Prayer first and *then* to engage in practical forms of outreach.

Early in 2018 we were thrilled to buy a little house three doors away from our worship centre. It took six months to refurbish and move in, and another five before we had our first housemate, but most days now, the morning begins with one of our community simply ministering to the Lord in the worship room. Our team is growing slowly. We are learning to love slow: in our experience, slow usually means sustainable, and we are definitely going after sustainable. Deep roots mean a strong tree. We want a hundred-year vision!

What's next?

If this is something which resonates with you, why not try your own experiment? Take a deep breath and get going – slowly at first. Commit yourself for the long haul and decide not to care about numbers. Try things. Don't get stressed if they do not work. Reflect, pray and ponder. Learn from what went well and what did not, then try again. Repeat! Lots!

Above all, let's not get so caught up in pursuing a vision that we forget to pursue Him. He is the Beginning and the End, the Reason for it all, our First Love and our One Thing. His desire for us, His urgent heart cry for intimacy with His people, resounds through eternity, and is calling us today.

Notes

i. Sean Feucht & David Fritch, *Burn 24-7: A Collision of Vertical Worship and the Great Commission* (Burn 24-7, 2014), ch. 1

ii. For a more extensive history of 24-7 prayer in the church from the first century to the present day, see https://www.ihopkc.org/prayerroom/history (accessed 28 May 2019)

CHAPTER 8

HEAVEN ON EARTH – THE POWER OF AGREEMENT

'If two believers on earth agree [that is, are of one mind, in harmony] about anything they ask [within the will of God], it will be done for them by My Father in heaven.'
Matthew 18:19 (AMP)

Every activity in the Tabernacle of David was about agreement. The whole enterprise was about bringing into being on the earth something which already existed in the heavens. David had glimpsed a heavenly eternal reality and created it in time and space; he caused the earth to line up with heaven. He also created a culture where it was normal for people from different families and tribes to walk together in agreement. Worship does that! When we agree about the worth, the glory, the majesty, and the beauty of Jesus, then our differences somehow cease to matter.

Teach us to pray

In Luke 11:1, before Jesus teaches His disciples on prayer, we read that He Himself had been praying. The implication is that it was in the hearing of the disciples. Then one of them asked Him, 'Please teach us to pray.' It is a strange request when you think about it; the disciples were all Jewish and presumably had been brought up with prayer as a normal part of life. It is as if the emphasis is not so much on 'Teach us to *pray*', but on 'Teach *us* to pray.' There was something about the way Jesus prayed that was different and compelling. They wanted to be able to pray like He did.

When Jesus instructs us to pray, 'Your kingdom come, Your will be done, *on earth as it is in heaven*' (Matthew 6:10, emphasis ours), He opens up the way for us to partner with God by taking time to see things from a heavenly perspective and then to live it out. Jesus lived this way Himself, explaining it to the disciples: 'Truly, truly, I say to you, the Son can do nothing of His own accord, but only what He sees the Father doing. For whatever the Father does, the Son does likewise' (John 5:19). It is easy to imagine Jesus' nights of prayer being taken up with allowing the Father to show Him what was going on in heaven, and then the next day being occupied with bringing it into being.

Intimacy Facilitates Agreement

Let's look again at the first couple of lines of the Lord's Prayer:

Our Father in heaven,
hallowed be Your Name
Your kingdom come, Your will be done,
on earth as it is in heaven.

Matthew 6:9-10

The prayer begins with an invitation to relationship and intimacy: 'Our *Father*' reveals God's heart for intimacy with us as part of His family. He is our Abba Father, our Papa, the One to whom we can draw close, whose love we can know and experience (Romans 8:15, Galatians 4:6). The prayer Jesus taught His disciples opens with this revelation. God is not distant and far off, but up close and personal.

Intimacy with the Father brings us into deeper intimacy with one another. Abba Father is *ours,* not mine. God's family has billions of children. This is a prayer to be prayed together with others. We can only pray it effectively if we agree with each other. And we do! How many cross-denominational gatherings are centred around praying the Lord's Prayer together? It is a constant point of agreement.

From the place of intimacy with God and our brothers and sisters, the prayer then continues into the place of agreement between heaven and earth: 'on earth as it is in heaven'. There is so much in that phrase. He does not intend us to pray blindly, not knowing anything about what is going on in heaven, but we pray with open eyes, ears and hearts. He wants to show us what heaven is like and how His will is being done there, so that we can establish it on the earth. As we pray the prayer together, we seek to learn from each other's perspectives and enter into the full counsel of our Father's will for the situations we face.

Worship Facilitates Unity

Agreement is very powerful. When we choose to live together in unity – actively going after it, and doing what we can to facilitate it – we live in a place of *commanded* blessing.

Behold how good and pleasant it is for brothers to dwell together in unity! . . . For there the Lord has commanded the blessing.

Psalm 133:1-3

Every time I read this, it causes me to ask what more I can do to live in unity with my brothers and sisters. How can I posture myself, and how can I relate intentionally with other believers in such a way that the Lord will *command* His blessing?

Those of us who grew up in a family with one or more siblings will understand that brothers and sisters do not always agree.

Agreement is often a choice to prize a relationship above an issue. Sometimes it takes brave communication to resolve conflict, and occasionally it may mean agreeing to disagree and yet still walk together.

How fascinating that this whole Psalm is written in the context of worship – the oil upon Aaron's head and robe, and the dew coming down on the hills of Zion! Worship always facilitates unity. That's why there is such a battle over it. I once heard Tiffany Buhler, the Managing Director of David's Tent, speak about unity and worship. What she said still provokes me:

'Worship is the single most important thing in bringing about unity. The most intimate thing we can do together is adore and love the Creator.'

If we allow ourselves to be open and intimate with the Lord in corporate worship, others will see us at our most vulnerable. Maybe that's why we all like to worship in our little ghettos – we feel safer that way. But if we are brave enough to step out of our comfort zones, the prize is huge. *Commanded* blessing! Don't we want to see our Father's heart explode with love for His children as they choose to worship together and walk with each other? Don't we long to experience the kind of unity which displays His love and grace to a watching world? How can we not at least try?

If we try to agree on *how* to worship before we begin, it will simply be divisive because we'll never agree. In our house, it can take over half an hour for us even to decide which movie to watch! We need to get away from fruitless discussions about preferred styles and just get on with it. The beauty of 24-7 worship and prayer is that different 'sets' can be taken by different people *in their own style.* You cannot do that in forty minutes, but you can in twelve or twenty-four hours. In recent years in Chester, we have been so blessed to experience city-wide extended times of prayer which have included Anglican daily offices, contemplative soaking, charismatic praise, focused and structured prayer times, children's sessions and intercessory worship. The opportunity to experience each other's styles and to develop a corporate sound in our city has been invaluable. It is only when we start to come together from across a city that we will discover our city's sound.

Wherever Two or Three Agree – the *Ekklesia*

Look at Matthew 18:19-20:

> If two of you agree on earth about anything they ask, it will be done for them by My Father in heaven. For where two or three are gathered in My Name, there am I among them.

Jesus' teaching here is in the context of the church as the *ekklesia* (see Matthew 18:17). In Roman times, the *ekklesia* had an important function, which it is vital for us to grasp if we are to understand the ramifications of what He is saying. It was a secular institution, a group of civic leaders, with authority to legislate in a city. So Jesus' listeners would have understood and experienced the *ekklesia* as a *governmental* body. In Matthew 16:18, Jesus' comment that He would establish His *ekklesia* was effectively a statement about *setting up a new form of government.*

In his book, *Ekklesia*, Ed Silvoso describes the *ekklesia's* existence in 'different forms and sizes', one of which was the *Conventus Civium Romanorum*. This was a group of Roman citizens, as few as two or three, whose 'coming together as fellow citizens automatically brought the power and presence of Rome into their midst.'[i] So wherever two or three members of a Roman *ekklesia* were present, they carried the full authority of Rome. It is fascinating to consider that, in Matthew 18:20 when He mentions 'two or three' believers, Jesus is alluding to the *Conventus.* Whenever two or three members of Jesus' *ekklesia* are gathered and agreed, *He is present with us and the full authority of heaven is behind us.*

Imagine a time of prayer where:

- we take time together to ask the Father about what He is doing in the heavenly eternal realm, then

- we come into faith agreement with Him and each other to see it come into being on the earth, and

- we pray, knowing we have authority to see things change.

That makes praying fun and effective! When we come into agreement with God and with each other, nothing is impossible.

Prayer is an Umbrella

As our vision to establish a place of night and day worship began to take shape, we decided to call it Presence House of Prayer. In recent months, as we have started to cast vision for our House of Prayer, we have been asked more than once, 'Oh, so aren't you doing worship any more then?' It is an understandable question, because we have tended to consider prayer and worship as two different things. In many settings, gatherings for 'prayer' and gatherings for 'worship' are entirely separate. But the 'House of Prayer' is a biblical concept, and has always included worship as well as prayer. Isaiah 56:7 in the Message translation puts in beautifully:

> I'll bring them to my holy mountain
> and give them joy in my house of prayer.
> They'll be welcome to worship the same as the 'insiders,'
> to bring burnt offerings and sacrifices to my altar.
> Oh yes, my house of worship
> will be known as a house of prayer for all people.

We have found it increasingly helpful to see 'Prayer' as an umbrella covering many different aspects of communion and communication with God.

We love Mahesh & Bonnie Chavda's description:

> We define prayer as communion with God . . . prayer
> is like a large tent that holds under it other aspects

83

of communion with Him . . . prayer is really drawing near to God and being with Him.[ii]

Different Types of Prayer Mean Different Types of Agreement

There are so many different types of prayer mentioned in the Bible. A quick search for the word 'prayer' in a Bible study app returned 114 mentions across the scriptures, with original Greek and Hebrew words meaning, amongst other things, intercession, devotion, supplication, and worship.

If we read through the Psalms, we find a rich diversity of different types of prayer, including worship, praise, thanksgiving and intercession. The beautiful prophetic song which David gave to Asaph for the tabernacle is a great example. See 1 Chronicles 16:7-36:

- **Worship** – 'Worship the Lord in the splendour of holiness.' (v. 29)

- **Praise** – 'Sing to Him, sing praises to Him; tell of all His wondrous works!' (v. 9)

- **Thanksgiving** – 'Oh give thanks to the Lord, for He is good; for His steadfast love endures for ever!' (v. 34)

- **Intercession** – 'Save us, O God of our salvation, and gather and deliver us from among the nations.' (v. 35)

Prophecy was also key for Asaph and his team (1 Chronicles 25:2), and there are numerous prophecies in the Psalms which are quoted in the Gospels and Acts (e.g. Acts

2:25-31). Fast forward to the New Testament, and we are encouraged to 'pray at all times in the Spirit, with all prayer and supplication' (Ephesians 6:18), and to make 'supplications, prayer, intercessions and thanksgiving . . . for all people' (2 Timothy 2:1).

It is not our purpose to make an exhaustive list of different types of prayer; rather, we hope that this provides a starting point and whets your appetite to go on your own journey of discovery with the Holy Spirit. The essential thing to note, however, is that every type of prayer has two vital things in common:

- Prayer is effective when it comes from the place of intimacy.

- Prayer establishes agreement.

Here are some examples of different types of prayer, together with their points of agreement:

- Worship – Agreement with God's desire for intimacy

- Praise – Agreement with God's nature

- Thanksgiving – Agreement with what God has done

- Intercession – Agreement with what God is doing

- Prophecy – Agreement with what God is going to do

- Supplication & Petition – Agreement that God is a good Father

- Declaration – Agreement with truth God has revealed

- Prayer in the Spirit – Agreement that we are dependent upon a supernatural God

Many of these types of prayer are interrelated and, in both personal and corporate prayer, we switch from one to the other without realising. For example, we have tried having some prayer times which are focused solely on praise, and it is incredible how quickly we switch to thanksgiving. It is almost impossible to separate intercession and prophecy, although there is a distinction between the two, because one informs and releases the other. However, in order to mine out some hidden treasures, we will take a look at them separately in the next chapter. We will consider the place of intimacy from which each springs, and the power of agreement that each represents.

Notes

i. Ed Silvoso, *Ekklesia: Rediscovering God's Instrument for Global Transformation* (Chosen Books, 2014), ch. 1

ii. Mahesh and Bonnie Chavda, *Watch of the Lord: The Secret Weapon of the Last-Day Church* (Creation House, 1999), ch. 3

CHAPTER 9

INTIMACY AND AGREEMENT
IN PRAYER

'Likeness was made for the purpose of
fellowship – intimate communion . . .
He longs for partnership. He risked
everything to have that one treasure.' [i]
Bill Johnson

David Was a Priest Before He Was a King

David understood the desire in God's heart for intimacy.
He was a teenager when Samuel pulled him out from
amongst his brothers and anointed him king over
Israel. It was years of hardship, pain and confusion later
when he actually stepped into the reality of the call. It
would have been understandable if he had wanted to
arrange for a lavish coronation immediately to assert his
authority and position, and yet what he did was to strip
off his clothing, don the garments of a priest and cause
himself to become completely undignified in a crazy
mess of sacrificial blood, noise and extravagant worship
(see 1 Chronicles 15:27-29).

David understood that his highest calling was that of
priestly ministry *to the Lord*, and that his kingship – the
authority to legislate heaven's agenda on the earth –
would follow. In his life, intimacy preceded agreement. He
was a priest before he was a king.

All Fruitfulness Flows From Intimacy

These verses in John's gospel say it all:

> Abide in me, and I in you. As the branch cannot bear fruit by itself, unless it abides in the vine, neither can you, unless you abide in me. I am the vine; you are the branches. Whoever abides in me and I in him, he it is that bears much fruit, for apart from me you can do nothing.
>
> *John 15:4-5*

We have to abide *in* Him before we can bear any fruit *for* Him. It is the only way. Heidi Baker has been a missionary in Mozambique for nearly twenty-five years. In that time, she and her husband Rolland have seen incredible miracles, including healings of deaf, blind and lame people, documented resurrections and multiplication of food. What is her strategy for dealing with the impossible demands they face every day? Abide in the secret place with the Lord because 'all fruitfulness flows from intimacy'.[ii]

Intimacy is at the very heart of agreement with God. We cannot come into agreement with Him unless we know Him, really know Him. This kind of knowing comes as a result of taking time in His presence. We cannot get to know Him overnight any more than we would know well a person we had only just met. We come to know Him over time spent intentionally in that pursuit. The Greek word for 'know', *ginosko*, used in a relational sense throughout the New Testament, carries the sense of a real heart knowledge, which leads to intimacy and takes time to develop.[iii]

Agreement and intimacy co-exist in beautiful synergy, fuelling and giving life to each other.

> Can two walk together unless they be agreed?
>
> *Amos 3:3 (KJV)*

We walk in intimacy with the Lord and come into agreement with Him. As we walk in agreement with Him, we find our intimacy with Him deepens.

In all the different types of prayer we could possibly pray, the key is relational intimacy with God. Coming to know Him involves learning what moves Him, and coming to understand the things that are on His heart for our own lives, and the people and situations He has positioned us to influence. Out of our intimacy with Him comes knowledge and understanding of His heart, and out of that revelation of His heart comes agreement as we choose to align ourselves with His will.

With this in mind, let us take a look at some different types of prayer.

Worship: Agreement With God's Desire For Intimacy

Worship is actually an extraordinarily prophetic act. We cannot worship if we do not believe God wants us close to Him, since worship is itself all about intimacy.

The most incredible thing about the tabernacle of David was that, as well as establishing night and day worship in the nation, it was a place of complete openness and access to God's presence. In David's tent, all could come all the time; people could come close. That has always been God's heart – to walk with His children like He did in the garden. He desires intimacy with us.

The biggest effect of the Fall was to separate us from that intimacy. How grieved must the Father have been when it happened? He has gone to every length possible to restore what was lost. The death and resurrection of Jesus have brought us back into that place of heart-to-heart relationship with Him. It makes the period of open access in David's tent even more incredible when we realise the grace of God in allowing that prophetic statement before the cross.

When we worship, we come into agreement with this incredible desire of God. We set everything else aside and simply come to be with Him, for His own sake, just because He wants us to come. There is nothing to ask, nothing to pray, maybe not as much to say or sing as we sometimes think. We rest in the incredible truth of open access to His heart.

When we choose to worship in the face of difficulty and challenge, we make a prophetic statement that we are refusing to let our circumstances come between us and God. We establish that we are one with Jesus in the middle of the storm. We declare that nothing can separate us from His love (Romans 8:35-39). His love remains. Circumstances can only bring separation if we let them. Worship brings us back into the place of oneness.

Listen to the words of David's tabernacle song:

Seek His face for evermore . . . Oh worship the Lord in the beauty of holiness.

1 Chronicles 16:11, 29 (KJV)

We cannot seek His face unless we come close. It is an invitation to draw near, to be transfixed by His beauty, enthralled by every feature. This is the same God who said to Moses, 'You cannot see my face and live' (Exodus 33:20). There is a prefiguring of the New Covenant here. We seek His face at the cost of our own lives. They are not worth holding onto in the light of His glory.

The Hebrew word for 'worship' in these verses is *shachah*. It means 'to bow yourself down, to crouch, to fall down flat'. In David's tabernacle, we are the sacrifice. We lay down our lives for the prize of knowing Him, beholding Him. And we worship in the beauty of *His* holiness – another cry from His heart for intimacy. He wants us to be with Him where He is (John 17:24), to clothe us with Himself (Galatians 3:27), to stretch His covering over us (Ruth 3:9).

The word for 'evermore' is *tamid*. It means 'perpetual', or 'continual daily employment'. This call to intimacy is our lifestyle now; it is who we are as believers. And when we take time out simply to worship, we make a prophetic declaration of that truth. We are one with Him, and He is worth it all.

Praise: Agreement with God's Nature

Praise is so powerful. Every time we praise God, we choose to celebrate an aspect of His nature. We come into agreement with the truth of who He is *no matter what the circumstances*.

At midnight, the darkest part of the night, in the inner dungeon, the darkest part of the prison, having been stripped, beaten with rods and shackled with their feet in stocks, Paul and Silas were 'singing hymns of praise to God' (Acts 16:25). How much physical pain must they have been in? To how much fear of their lives could they have surrendered? How much reason did they have to judge and condemn those who had hurt them? How much could they have chosen to blame God for their predicament? But what did they choose to do? They *chose* to *praise*.

What is He like? He is good, faithful, kind, loving, beautiful, wonderful, awesome, powerful, glorious, merciful and great. That's just the start. The list of His attributes is endless! We can choose any one of them and start to praise Him, whatever is going on around us. We do not just praise Him in the good times. Every challenging circumstance provides us with an opportunity to praise Him in a way we could never do otherwise. When we choose to praise Him in the middle of bereavement, loss, pain, confusion, illness and financial hardship, we put on praise as a garment (Psalms 33:1) and take a stand on the truth of who He is. There is no better choice when faced with things we do not understand.

The weapons of our warfare are spiritual (see 2 Corinthians 10:4). 'Our weapon is a melody,' as Jonathan and Melissa Helser declare in their song *Raise a Hallelujah*.[iv] We read about times when the singers went ahead of the army in ancient Israel and brought about great victories as they praised (2 Chronicles 20:21-22). Praise and declaration are key. Words are creative. As we sing praises, we establish truth ahead of us that we can enter into. Praise opens prison doors, breaks chains, causes walls to fall, calms storms and shifts spiritual atmospheres. The circumstances in our lives do not change who He is; our praise changes the circumstances.

Thanksgiving: Agreement with What God Has Done

It is a good and delightful thing to give thanks to the Lord.

Psalm 92:1 (AMP)

Enter His gates with a song of thanksgiving
And His courts with praise
Be thankful to Him, bless and praise His name.

Psalm 100:4 (AMP)

Thanksgiving reminds us about what He has done and encourages us that He can and will do it again. Giving thanks opens up gates in the heavenly realms and gives us access to deeper and higher places. But thanksgiving is not simply a 'password' for us to use to open these gates. How can we come empty-handed before the King? What better gift to give Him than our thanks? It is good for us to fill our hearts and hands with thankfulness and come ready to pour out to Him of the goodness He has given.

And now we thank You, our God, and praise Your glorious name . . . For all things come from You and of Your own have we given You.

1 Chronicles 29:13-14

Our Father is so blessed when we acknowledge His heart of love in the gifts He gives. Gratitude even provides an antidote to disappointment and confusion; we can't dwell on good stuff and bad stuff at the same time.

Worship, praise and thanksgiving are all aspects of prayer with which we can engage regardless of circumstance. They are all focused on the Lord and who He is, not on circumstances or human emotion, which can change. How many times have we all prayed something like 'Lord, I thank You that You are able to . . .?' This kind of thanksgiving pulls our eyes towards Him, and releases faith. In every gospel account of Jesus feeding the 5,000 and 4,000, the first thing He did after taking the loaves was to give thanks (e.g. John 6:11). Thanksgiving brought about multiplication and miracles of abundance. It changed situations and lives.

I gave my life to Jesus when I was ten years old. Within a week, I had started to read *The Hiding Place* by Corrie ten Boom.[v] It is not the kind of book you usually give a ten-year-old, but I am so glad someone gave it to me. At the beginning of my walk with Jesus, it convinced me that there was nothing too hard or too dark for Him, and that I could give thanks whatever was going on around. I was inspired by stories of His faithfulness and grace in the direst of situations. On one occasion, Corrie's sister Betsie encouraged her to give thanks for being sent into a barracks full of fleas. Corrie resisted, but Betsie reminded her about 1 Thessalonians 5:18, which tells us to 'give thanks in all circumstances'. So, through gritted teeth, Corrie did so, and entered into a remarkable miracle of protection in which many people came to faith. (The fleas kept the Nazi guards away so that Corrie and Betsie could preach the gospel unhindered.)

It is so good to remind ourselves about how much the Lord has done for us, and to take time to thank Him. It is something we often forget to do. We take what He has given and run. We can become so complacent about His blessings. It is our responsibility to remind ourselves about His blessings and to choose to give thanks for them:

Bless and affectionately praise the Lord, O my soul.
And do not forget any of His benefits.

Psalm 103:2 (AMP)

When I was a child, my mum used to insist on Boxing Day being spent writing thank-you letters to relatives who had sent me presents. All I wanted to do was play! But Mum was right. It is good to give thanks! It acknowledges the value of the gift, the love of the person who gave it, and so releases us to enjoy it fully. Thanksgiving is a discipline, a habit to be learned, but it is a source of great joy.

Intercession: Agreement with What God is Doing

It is important to remember that all intercessory prayer is done in the context of Christ's work of intercession. Jesus Himself is the Chief Intercessor – and the primary result of His intercession for us is intimacy:

Consequently, He is able to save to the uttermost *those who draw near to God through Him*, since He always lives to make intercession for them.

Hebrews 7:25 (emphasis ours)

Intercession comes from intimacy. It has to. We have to get close, we have to press in to know Him if we are to understand the things that are on His heart and how He wants us to pray. If we take time to simply *be* with the Lord, to get to know Him and understand His heart, then we will surely begin to pray in line with His will. In her book *The Happy Intercessor,* Beni Johnson describes her journey:

Intercession is just the fruit of being with Him. It was birthed in my own heart because of spending time with Him.[vi]

The Lord shared with Abraham, His *friend,* what He was about to do (Genesis 18:17); Abraham was then released into a *dialogue* of intercession with Him. Abraham was not battling against God, not trying to twist His arm, but partnering with Him. God drew Abraham into a conversation. That's what He desires for us as well.

When we intercede, we 'stand in the gap' on behalf of the people for whom we are praying; we bring alignment between heaven and earth. The Hebrew word for intercession, *paga,* carries both the sense of a face-to-face meeting, and the role of standing alongside others to help lift and carry away their burdens.[vii] We meet with the Father, bringing to Him the cares and concerns we have about family, friends, our cities and nations, and then we release His desires on the earth as we enter into agreement with Him.

In his book, *Secrets of a Prayer Warrior*, Derek Prince summarises it beautifully:

> The intercessor is God-centred. He is not problem-focused; he is not focused on what man can or cannot do. He has a vision of what God can do. ... [An intercessor] must have an intimate acquaintance with God.[viii]

Intercessory worship is giving fresh impetus to prayer in many Houses of Prayer. This is a form of combined musical worship and prayer. As people pray, the leader listens to catch key themes or phrases, and then turns them into simple responsive songs so that the intercession can become corporate. We find that as we gather to lift up the name of Jesus, to minister to Him, He opens His heart and reveals His purposes and plans to us. This releases us into intercession to see His will done on the earth. When we feel the burden of intercession lift, we find ourselves propelled into worship again. Sometimes all the Lord wants is our time. When we press beyond the usual thirty to forty minutes of worship and 'waste' our precious resource of time on Him, we enter into experiences and insights which can come no other way.

Prophecy: Agreement with What God is Going to Do

I remember vividly the excitement of learning how to prophesy. As a teenager in the 1980s I was blessed to be part of different churches where, in small groups, we spent ages worshipping and 'waiting on God', receiving simple pictures and trying to interpret them to discover what He was saying. It was incredible to think that God actually wanted to share His heart with us! We learned to receive His encouragement through one another, and to develop a sense of where He was leading us individually and corporately. In the 1990s and 2000s, we were privileged to receive amazing teaching from tested and tried prophetic people from all over the world, developing and honing our ability to hear what the Lord is saying. It is important, though, that we do not spend all our time in prophetic conferences; life is not one big prophetic activation! It is still fun to prophesy, but it is also sobering and weighty.

The one who prophesies speaks to people for edification for their upbuilding and encouragement and consolation . . . the one who prophesies builds up the church.

1 Corinthians 14:3-4

The Bible is clear that 'all can prophesy' (1 Corinthians 14:31) and that we should 'eagerly desire' this precious gift (1 Corinthians 14:39). We desire the gift of prophecy because the Lord desires to share His heart with us. Prophecy allows us to understand His desires, to release and speak them out, and bring things into alignment in people's lives and the situations around us.

Learning to prophesy is like learning a new language – it comes in fits and starts with lots of mistakes, simply at first, and then more fluently – and we get better the more we practise, and the more help and support we get. There are countless books and podcasts to help us, but they will all be useless without intimacy with Him. We draw close; we seek to see, to hear, to understand. As we do so, the Lord reveals His will to us. He uncovers His heart and trusts us with His vulnerability.

The Lord God does nothing without revealing His secret to His servants, the prophets.

Amos 3:7

Prophecy releases hope because it speaks into the future. It is a promise, not a prediction. Prophecy demands from us action and response. It draws us into even deeper intimacy as we seek to partner with the Lord and posture our hearts and lives to come into line with what He is revealing about the way we should go. This is true for both corporate and personal words of prophecy.

For example, as we gather to worship across a city, the Lord may begin to speak to us about His heart to deal with disunity amongst believers. He may even reveal that this disunity has a root in some kind of spiritual stronghold. Weighing this word against Scripture, we can come into agreement with heaven and with each other that it is good and true. But if we sit around waiting for the Lord to intervene sovereignly, or even just pray about it, we will have missed it. We also need to posture our lives towards increased unity with brothers and sisters and press into the Lord for wisdom, strength and grace to walk differently in practical ways. This might be as simple as getting coffee with someone to develop a friendship, or having a conversation and asking good questions with a goal of understanding someone better.

Pressing into prophecy in this way will always cost us, but it is so worth it! It drives us deeper into the Lord because we simply do not have the capacity in ourselves to walk it out. And as we go deeper, He reveals His heart to us again and again, drawing us deeper still.

Supplication and Petition: Agreement That God is a Good Father

The Greek word, *deesis*, is variously translated *supplication* or *petition.* It carries the sense of a request or entreaty, a 'felt need that is both personal and urgent'.[ix] For example, it is found in both of these well-known verses:

> With all prayer and *petition* pray at all times in the Spirit
>
> *Ephesians 6:18 (NASB, emphasis ours)*

> Do not be anxious about anything, but in everything by prayer and *supplication* with thanksgiving let your requests be made known to God.
>
> *Philippians 4:6 (emphasis ours)*

If you think about it, prayers of petition and supplication are the kinds of prayers we pray all the time without really thinking, sometimes with greater urgency or intensity when the need is more pressing. How many times a day do we find ourselves saying, 'Oh Lord, please . . .'? Every time we pray this way, we come into agreement with the fact that God is a good Father. We ask Him because we believe He cares and is able to do something about the things we are asking Him for. If we do not believe that, there is no point in asking!

Over and over again in Scripture we are encouraged to ask:

> Ask and it will be given to you . . . How much more will your Father in heaven give good things to those who ask Him.
>
> *Matthew 7:7, 11*

> If two of you on earth agree about anything you ask it will be done for them by my Father in heaven.
>
> *Matthew 18:19*

> You do not have because you do not ask.
>
> *James 4:2*

Our Father wants us to ask on behalf of ourselves, our families and friends, our communities, cities, nation. I love how the Message Translation puts 2 Timothy 1:2: 'Pray every way you know how for everyone you know.'

Again, it is all about intimacy, all about desire. We are told to ask according to His will:

This is the confidence that we have towards Him, that if we ask anything according to His will He hears us.

1 John 5:14

What is his will? Let us ask Him. He knows what we need before we even ask, even when we do not know what we need ourselves. We think we know what is best, but often we are not sure. As we take time with Him, He helps us to understand ourselves better and gives us insight into the nature of our need so that we can pray out of faith and peace rather than out of fear, pain or confusion.

There are other powerful tools of supplication at our disposal: God has revealed His will in the Scriptures so we can pray from the Bible by asking the Lord to highlight promises in specific verses and then turning them into prayers. Praying in tongues is also great because when we use our spiritual prayer language we always pray in line with His will (Romans 8:26).

Perhaps the greatest prayer of petition we can ever pray is recorded in Luke 11:12:

How much more will the heavenly Father give the Holy Spirit to those who ask Him?

What an incredible prayer! As we pray this, our wonderful Father gives His Holy Spirit without measure, the Holy

Spirit leads us deeper into Jesus who is the Truth (John 16:13), and Jesus reveals the Father to us (Luke 10:22) – so we have increased confidence and faith to ask the Father for more. What a glorious unending cycle of petition and supplication, bringing us into deeper intimacy and agreement with Him.

Declaration: Agreement with Truth God Has Revealed

Prayers of declaration are inextricably linked with prophetic revelation. They are an incredibly powerful form of agreement. Look at these scriptural precedents:

> For Zion's sake I will not keep silent . . . you shall be called by a new name . . . You shall no more be termed Forsaken, and your land shall no more be termed Desolate, but you shall be called My Delight Is in Her, and your land Married.
>
> *Isaiah 62:1-4*

> And I tell you, you are Peter, and on this rock I will build My church.
>
> *Matthew 16:18*

Just think how declarations like this changed the destinies of individuals and nations as they were declared out loud and penetrated the hearts of the hearers! Jabez changed his own future by declaring truth over himself and refusing to accept that he was destined to live in pain (the meaning of his name) (1 Chronicles 4:9, 10). David was not encouraging himself into a reckless act by asking 'Who is this uncircumcised Philistine?' about

Goliath (1 Samuel 17:26). He was declaring truth and shifting the atmosphere to change the destiny of a nation as he declared who God was. How safe and affirmed must Timothy have felt to have been declared Paul's son (1 Timothy 1:18)? How must that have released him to be and do everything he was called to?

We can turn personal and corporate prophetic words into declarations of truth (1 Timothy 1:18). We can take hold of scriptures and declare them over ourselves, our friends and family members, workplaces, and other areas in which the Lord has given us influence and responsibility. Declaring revealed truth always displaces lies and brings us into agreement with heaven's agenda on the earth.

It is important to understand that we cannot simply declare anything and everything we fancy! But we can achieve so much in the place of prayer by taking time to discover our Father's will for specific situations, places and people and *declaring* it, as well as by allowing it to inform our prayers of intercession and petition. The Holy Spirit always leads us into increased truth (John 16:13), so deepening our relationship with Him and pursuing greater intimacy will cause us to come into greater revelation of the Lord's will.

Behold, you delight in truth in the inward being, and you teach me wisdom in the secret heart.

Psalm 51:6

Knowing that we know His heart will give us increased confidence to declare the truths He reveals and bring things around us into alignment with heaven's perspective.

Praying in the Spirit: Agreement That We Are Dependent Upon a Supernatural God

One of the first signs that the Father had given the promised gift of Holy Spirit Himself was that believers began to pray in tongues (see Acts 2:4; Acts 10:46). There is no closer agreement in prayer with God we can achieve than when we pray in tongues. When we pray in the Spirit we *always* pray in accordance with His will (Romans 8:26). The Holy Spirit Himself, living inside us, prays through us, as we use this mysterious and wonderful gift. Our spirit is perfectly in tune with Him. How awesomely intimate is that?

The previous sections in this chapter have all emphasised our need to develop our relationship with God so that we know His heart and therefore understand how to pray. We will most often pray along the right lines when we posture ourselves in this way, but we may not always get it right. When we pray in tongues, we simply lean into Him and let Him loose within us. Our minds are not engaged. We can't go wrong. It is so liberating to be able to say, 'I really have no idea how to pray in this situation, Lord, so would You just pray through me, please?' In fact, we almost entitled this section 'Agreement that we haven't a clue what we're doing!'

We remember the swirling debates around this incredible gift, and the focus and determination with which we prayed until we received it. In the late 80s, we spent home group meetings doing nothing but praying in tongues. And now we are probably among so many others who often neglect it, pull it out when things are desperate, or use it for a few minutes when we've run out of things to sing about in worship. How sad! Perhaps the phenomenal level of agreement this gift provides is why the enemy has tried so hard to shut it down – with controversy, apathy and distraction.

When we pray in tongues, we edify, or strengthen, our inner man (1 Corinthians 14:4). That's something we often neglect to do, but it is as important as making sure we look after our physical bodies. There are many scriptures which encourage us to do this (e.g. Ephesians 3:16, Colossians 1:11). The Lord also loves to give us interpretation of what we are praying or singing so that we can then pray more effectively in our native language (1 Corinthians 14:13).

As we determine to press beyond the two-minute 'wall' we can experience when praying in tongues, we often sense things shifting in the spiritual realm and simply 'know' that 'it is done'. Extended times of praying in tongues can also open up prophetic experiences and visions; as we pray in the Spirit, intimately connected with our Father's heart and will, He loves to open our eyes to fresh revelation.

Praying in tongues in an intercessory or petitionary way can be highly effective and exciting. In *Chasing the Dragon,* Jackie Pullinger talks about the wonderful miracles she experienced as a missionary in Hong Kong's infamous Walled City, after having decided to pray in tongues for just fifteen minutes a day. She saw such breakthrough that she began praying in the Spirit continually as she walked the streets. People who had been drug addicts for years were completely delivered as they prayed in tongues.[x] We once heard a testimony from someone who had been invited to advise people in very significant leadership positions. He had not sought the role, nor had he felt qualified. When he asked the Lord how it had happened, He answered, 'That's what you were asking for when you were praying in tongues for all that time each day!'

We are currently convicted about the need to get this gift out of its box, dust it off and use it again – deliberately and regularly. Maybe we'll try a whole worship set when we do nothing else!

What an Invitation!

These truths about intimacy and agreement are fundamentally an invitation into a journey – deeper into the Lord's heart, and more fully into an experience of partnering with Him in seeing His Kingdom established on the earth. What an honour! What a privilege! What an invitation! Hundreds of thousands of hearts across the globe are joining in a resounding 'Yes!'. Will you join them?

Notes

i. Bill Johnson, *Hosting the Presence: Unveiling Heaven's Agenda* (Destiny Image, 2012), ch. 2

ii. See, for example, Heidi Baker, *Birthing the Miraculous: The Power of Personal Encounters with God to Change Your Life and the World* (Charisma House Book Group, 2014), ch. 3

iii. https://www.biblestudytools.com/lexicons/greek/nas/ginosko.html (accessed 28 May 2019)

iv. See here for the full story of how powerful this song has been in the healing of a little boy – https://www.youtube.com/watch?v=awkO61T6i0k (accessed 28 May 2019)

v.   Corrie ten Boom with John and Elizabeth Sherrill, *The Hiding Place* (Hodder and Stoughton, 1972). This book describes Corrie ten Boom's story. During the Nazi occupation of the Netherlands in World War II, Corrie's family hid Jews in a secret room in their home. They were eventually betrayed and sent to concentration camps where her sister, Betsie, died.

vi.   Beni Johnson, *The Happy Intercessor* (Destiny Image, 2009), ch. 2

vii. For a fuller discussion of these aspects of intercession, see Dutch Sheets, *Intercessory Prayer: How God Can Use Your Prayers to Move Heaven and Earth* (Regal Books, 1996), chs. 4 & 5

viii. Derek Prince, *Secrets of a Prayer Warrior* (Derek Prince Ministries International, 2009), ch. 4

ix.   https://biblehub.com/greek/1162.htm (accessed 28 May 2019)

x.   Jackie Pullinger and Andrew Quicke, *Chasing the Dragon* (Hodder and Stoughton, 1980). This book tells Jackie's story of ministry among drug addicts, prostitutes and criminals in Kowloon, Hong Kong's Walled City.

CHAPTER 10

WE HAVE COME TO MOUNT ZION

'When we worship, we have access
to the heavenly realm.' [i]
Beni Johnson

A few years ago, I (Robin) experienced a paradigm shift regarding worship.

We were in a small gathering, beginning with a time of worship. As our friend was 'kicking off' the meeting, he commented how we often invite God to come into our midst, or tell Him that He is welcome among us. Then he invited us to see things from God's perspective – it was the other way round! As we began to worship, *He* was welcoming *us* into *His* Presence. One by one we were appearing before Him in His throne room. I realised that this is a scriptural way of looking at things. The Psalmist describes a group of people with worshipping hearts and says:

Each one appears before God in Zion.

Psalm 84:7

As we have already seen, Zion is not just a physical mountain. It also describes a spiritual reality, a place where we meet with God and join with thousands of others, both people and angels, to worship Him in Spirit and truth:

You have not come to a mountain that can be touched . . . you have come to Mount Zion, to the city of the living God, the heavenly Jerusalem. You have come to thousands upon thousands of angels in joyful assembly, to the church of the firstborn, whose names are written in heaven. You have come to God, the Judge of all, to the spirits of the righteous made perfect, to Jesus the mediator of a new covenant, and to the sprinkled blood that speaks a better word than the blood of Abel.

Hebrews 12:18-24 (NIV)

What happened in David's time, on Mount Zion, was a foretaste of something we can all experience today. There is a heavenly reality for us to enter into.

Seeing the Invisible

For many years, I struggled in times of worship. Sometimes I would feel that I was able to 'connect' with God, but in general it felt very hit and miss. My problem was that I was easily distracted. I found it easier to get caught up with what was going on around me than to focus on God.

I do not think my experience is unusual. Although the things of God are of infinite value, they are invisible. And all the time our senses are being bombarded by the world around us. The things of this world may only be 'temporal', but they are visible and touchable, audible and smellable!

Focusing our attention on the unseen realm can feel like a battle. But it is a battle God intends us to win. The Holy Spirit encourages us to look not at the things which are seen, but at the things which are not seen; for the things which are seen are temporal, but the things which are not seen are eternal.

2 Corinthians 4:18 (NASB)

As we do so, He promises that our

momentary, light affliction is producing for us an eternal weight of glory far beyond all comparison.

2 Corinthians 4:17 (NASB)

Joining With the Heavenly Worship

Every time we worship, we have the privilege of entering into the heavenly worship that is pictured in the book of Revelation.[ii] This worship goes on around the clock – the twenty-four elders throwing their crowns down at the feet of Jesus; the four living creatures around the throne crying 'Holy!'; and

many angels, numbering myriads of myriads and thousands of thousands, saying with a loud voice, 'Worthy is the Lamb who was slain, to receive power and wealth and wisdom and might and honour and glory and blessing!'

Revelation 5:11-12

It is exciting to realise that we get to join in with this heavenly scene. The moment we engage our focus on God and begin to worship, we are appearing before His throne. I now often picture myself joining with those heavenly worshippers – the elders, the living creatures and the countless angels. This is a healthy way to use my imagination, because it really *is* happening! I really *am* appearing before God in Zion!

My experience has been transformed, and I now find it harder to be passive in worship. As I remember that I am joining in with the worship of heaven, I find a growing desire within myself to be demonstrative – to worship God 'with all my strength' – even though this has not always come naturally to me. It is an ongoing process, and for me a key has been to focus on worshipping Him 'with all my heart and with all my soul' (see Deuteronomy 6:5). As I do so, it is inevitable that, eventually, my body will be affected too! I find it often helps for me to just close my eyes, shut out all the distractions, and focus my attention on God; or to adopt a different posture, such as kneeling, lying prostrate or even dancing.

A Doorway to Heavenly Experiences

God truly is a Rewarder of those who earnestly seek Him (Hebrews 11:6). This chapter began with a great quote from Beni Johnson:

> When we worship, we have access to the heavenly realm.

In extended times of worship, we have discovered how exciting it can be to go on a journey of worship with the Holy Spirit as our Guide. We never know where He is going to take us or what He will show us. If there are a dozen people in the room, we may have twelve different experiences in His presence. One person may have a heavenly vision; another may receive a physical healing; somebody may receive a fresh revelation from a Bible verse; and someone else may just feel God's love flooding their whole being. On the other hand, there are powerful times when we all share in a corporate prophetic experience together.

We have found that God sometimes reveals truths to us, as we worship, that we would never have found out in a lifetime of study. 'For You to die was all about desire' is an example of this (see Chapter 1). We actually get revelation as we are singing. The Psalms describe this experience brilliantly:

I will break open mysteries with my music
And my song will release riddles solved.
Psalm 49:4 (TPT)

In a similar way, things we know in our heads can come alive in our hearts with a profound impact. I had a moment like this in a recent worship time. I already knew that 'the name of the Lord is a strong tower' (Proverbs 18:10). Then I had a moment in worship in which I could actually sense the Name of Jesus all around me. I felt as though I was inside a building, a place of incredible peace, where I knew I was totally safe. Having experienced this once, my perception of that verse is changed forever.

It is exciting to hear people's stories of heavenly experiences. I love Claire's account of the harp in her heart, which she shares in chapter two. There is so much more to explore in the heavenly realms – we have only begun to scratch the surface!

There is a challenge for us here. We do not worship our God in order to have these experiences. We worship Him because He is worthy. But we cannot deny that He blesses us when we worship Him. Each of us is responsible for stewarding our own heart, and for making sure that we continue to seek the Giver, not the good gifts that He gives.

We stay in a place of freedom by adopting a posture of surrender, which says, 'If He chooses to take us into heavenly realms, or to reveal profound truths to our hearts, then that is up to Him. But I am going to worship Him anyway, because He is worthy of all that I can give Him.' Our friend Rich di Castiglione sometimes asks this question, to help us keep our motivation pure, 'Would we worship Him if He never did another thing for us?'

We are Changed as We Worship

It is also inevitable that we will be transformed as we worship. The more we gaze upon His beauty, the more we become like Him.

> But we all, with unveiled face, beholding as in a mirror the glory of the Lord, are being transformed into the same image from glory to glory, just as from the Lord, the Spirit.
>
> *2 Corinthians 3:18 (NASB)*

This transformation takes place as we experience God's love for us afresh. He really, really wants us to experience His love. He doesn't just want us to know *by faith* that He loves us. He wants us to *feel* His love for us too:

> Hope does not disappoint us, because God's love has been poured into our hearts through the Holy Spirit that has been given to us.
>
> *Romans 5:5 (NRSV)*

It is the goal of God that we experience His love and affirmation. He wants to be our primary source of praise and encouragement. Then we are less prone to look for those things in other places.

As we worship, our spirits ascend and soar. Then we get a completely different perspective on the situations around us. I love what Bill Johnson says:

> 'I remember hearing Derek Prince speak on this subject about 40 years ago. It impacted me so profoundly. He said if you have ten minutes to pray, take about eight minutes for worship. It is amazing what you can pray for in two minutes.' [iii]

He is Always Worthy

You are worthy of it all
You are worthy of it all
For from You are all things
And to You are all things
You deserve the glory [iv]

Our worship experience is incomplete if we only worship God when we feel like it, or in order to feel good. I had a valuable lesson in this respect at David's Tent in 2016. It was the final morning and, after three days of extended worship and a night with virtually no sleep, I felt tired. My stamina was all used up. I was really just 'going through the motions'. Then, to my surprise, the worship leader stopped for a moment and asked us all if we were hungry for more of God. He lovingly invited us to repent from any lack of expectancy, and ask God for more hunger. I knew I needed to respond to this challenge!

Even though I was physically tired and losing my voice, I was inspired by the energy with which everyone around me was singing and dancing. I knew I could give God more too. After a while, we moved into a quieter song about pouring out our worship to Him. I knelt down with my head on the trampled grass. All of a sudden, I found myself sobbing. I did not really know what was happening, but it felt good. God was doing a deep work of healing in my heart. But I also learned that there are greater blessings stored up for us when we press beyond our feelings in worship. He is always worthy of our all.

Resetting the Bar

Another thing that happens when we worship is that we remember how good it is to be immersed in God's Presence. It is like resetting the bar. We see Him for who He really is; we see ourselves as He sees us; we remember how much He loves us; and we get His perspective afresh on situations we face.

Ultimately, our goal is to live like this all the time – abiding in His presence twenty-four-seven – which is why the Holy Spirit tells us continually to

> be filled with the Spirit, speaking to one another in psalms and hymns and spiritual songs, singing and making melody with your heart to the Lord.
>
> *Ephesians 5:18-19 (NASB)*

In the presence of the Lord, there is fullness of joy (Psalm 16:11). God is seated in the heavenlies and He laughs at His enemies (Psalm 2:4); and we are seated with Him in heavenly places in Jesus (Ephesians 2:6), which means that we can laugh at our enemies too.

I have not yet learned how to abide in that place all the time. But the more I worship Him, the more frequently I 'reset the bar' in my own heart – and remind myself of the deep peace that comes from resting in His love for me.

Worship Changes Atmospheres

Here is another quote that I love from Beni Johnson's book, The Happy Intercessor:

> When we worship, we can release the presence of God and His Kingdom into the room.[v]

This is so true! The whole atmosphere in the room changes when just one person worships Jesus with their whole heart. The story of Mary of Bethany is a beautiful picture of this:

> Mary then took a pound of very costly perfume of pure nard, and anointed the feet of Jesus and wiped His feet with her hair; and the house was filled with the fragrance of the perfume.
>
> *John 12:3 (NASB)*

It was not only the fragrance of the perfume that filled the house. The fragrance of Mary's worship filled the house too!

It is a delight to be in a room when there's a whole bunch of people worshipping like Mary. It is also powerful in terms of spiritual warfare. We do not even have to be thinking about our spiritual enemies, and yet our worship is effective in defeating them:

Let the high praises of God be in their mouth,
And a two-edged sword in their hand . . .
To bind their kings with chains
And their nobles with fetters of iron.

Psalm 149:6-8 (NASB)

Five of you will chase a hundred, and a hundred of you will chase ten thousand, and your enemies will fall before you by the sword.

Leviticus 26:8 (NASB)

These verses tell us that our worship and our praises are an essential element of our warfare, and that there is a multiplication effect.

You are holy, enthroned on the praises of Israel.

Psalm 22:3

When we worship, we are lifting up Jesus as King. As we recognise and proclaim His supreme authority, it weakens and undermines the power of other rulers and authorities. And this causes the spiritual atmosphere to shift. We may not be able to observe this taking place directly, but we *can* witness the changes that take place as a result.

Community Transformation

The Welsh Revival of 1904 provided dramatic examples of atmospheres shifting. As the Holy Spirit moved, tens of thousands worshipped passionately all over the country, and the impact was felt everywhere:

Even the most powerful politicians, statesmen, intellectuals, and rival religious leaders had difficulty denying the impact of the revival on the entire principality of Wales. Debts were paid, stolen goods returned, and the taverns were forsaken and closed. A serious problem developed at the mines because the horses had been trained to respond to commands that were curses from the drivers, and since drivers did not curse anymore, the horses could not understand their commands! [vi]

Recognising the way atmospheres are changed through worship, the Burn 24-7 movement intentionally combines worship and missions, in order to 'carry His Presence and joy to the darkest, hardest and most impossible places on earth'.[vii] The following testimony provides a beautiful example of the impact of worship in a Kurdish community living in a former Iraqi military base. Before the team began to worship, over a hundred people had been jostling and fighting. Jeremy Perigo writes:

We realised that unless something was done immediately, we were going to have a massive problem. A few of us grabbed our instruments and started worshipping . . . Suddenly, the crowd stopped fighting . . . After about an hour of worshipping, the Spirit of God began to fill these precious people with supernatural joy and hope as they began to sing, dance, and play their native drums. Indigenous sounds of freedom, joy, and hope began to rise up to the heavens. These Kurds, who were being touched by the Spirit, took over our worship set as they began to erupt in passionate, fresh, indigenous songs.[viii]

As we saw earlier, we are beginning to experience the transformative power of worship in our own city too. It is still early days, but we are convinced that the more we worship and pray, the more we will see lives, communities, and cities transformed by the love of God. He has done it before. We can't wait to see Him do it again!

Notes

i.   Beni Johnson, *The Happy Intercessor* (Destiny Image, 2009), ch. 8
ii.   See Revelation 4:1-5:14.
iii. Bill Johnson, *Hosting the Presence: Unveiling Heaven's Agenda* (Destiny Image, 2012), ch. 10
iv.   *Worthy of It All* by David Brymer and Ryan Hall © 2012 Common Hymnal Publishing, Innerland, Wayfinder Music, Underground Treasure
v.   Beni Johnson, *The Happy Intercessor* (Destiny Image, 2009), ch. 8
vi.   Rick Joyner, *The Power to Change the World* (MorningStar Publications, Inc., 2006), ch. 9
vii. www.burn24-7.com/missions, accessed on 30 May 2019
viii. Jeremy Perigo in Sean Feucht & David Fritch, *Burn 24-7: A Collision of Vertical Worship and the Great Commission* (Burn 24-7, 2014), ch. 7

CHAPTER 11

WASTE IT ALL

'None of us have an option when it comes to
whether or not our lives will be wasted. The only
option we have is how we will waste them ...
Jesus loves the world and the church, but there
is a special grace that He gives to those who
seek to love Him in an extravagant way,
to those who waste their lives on Him.'[i]

Mike Bickle

Hidden Treasure

God sometimes hides precious treasure in the most
unlikely places.

There is a wonderful revelation hidden away in Second
Chronicles. It is in the middle of a rebuke delivered to a
righteous king, Jehu, whose had heart had grown cold
towards God. Hanani the Seer said to him:

> For the eyes of the Lord move to and fro throughout
> the earth that He may strongly support those whose
> heart is completely His.
>
> *2 Chronicles 16:9 (NASB)*

Although Jehu had sinned, God was inviting him to
return to his first love. Tragically, he did not respond, but
hardened his heart. As a result, his life ended in dishonour.

An Invitation

The same invitation rings out from the heart of God to us. It is an invitation to extravagant devotion. And it comes with an incredible promise – that God will give us *His strong support* if we will love Him with all our heart.

Jesus restates this promise of powerful heavenly backing when He declares:

> Seek first the kingdom of God and his righteousness, and all these things will be added to you.
>
> *Matthew 6:33*

We are finding out that when something looks wholehearted and beautiful in God's eyes, it can often seem wasteful and excessive to many onlookers. If we are unrestrained in our devotion, we can expect criticism.

The woman who broke an alabaster jar, and poured out all her expensive perfume on Jesus, provides a vivid illustration of this. To extravagant worshippers, she is a hero and a role model. But there are still those who will say, 'Why this waste? For this could have been sold for a large sum and given to the poor' (Matthew 26:7-8).

The people who will change the world are the extravagant ones. It is their worship that will fill the world with the knowledge of the glory of God. So let us learn the language of excess – joyfully 'wasting' our time on Him – and experience what the strong support of God looks like.

Chris McClarney's song 'Waste It All' expresses it well:

> I want to waste it all on You
> I want to pour my heart's perfume
> I don't care if I'm called a fool
> I'm wasting it all on You.[ii]

God is not inviting us to be history-makers. He is inviting us to pursue intimacy with Him, and lavish time on Him when no one else is looking. As Chris Burns says:

> The greatest call of the Christian in these days is to walk with God in intimacy. [iii]

He is looking for lovers, not world-changers. It just so happens that He will use such people to change the world!

As we draw this book to a close, will you draw aside and incline your ear to the Holy Spirit's whisper? Can you hear Him inviting you? Do you hear Him say how much He loves it when you come, just to be with Him?

> Let Me see your face,
> Let Me hear your voice,
> For your voice is sweet,
> And your face is lovely.
> *Song of Songs 2:14*

Ask Him, 'What does it look like for me to follow in the footsteps of King David and Mary of Bethany? Show me what it looks like for my heart to be completely Yours. Teach me how to live a life of delighting myself in You!'

Then wait quietly before Him and see what He says.

Notes

i. Mike Bickle, *Passion for Jesus* (Charisma House, 2007), ch. 17

ii. *Waste It All* by Chris McClarney, Christa Black, Laura Rhinehart © 2010 Capitol CMG Paragon, Jesus Culture Music Group, Thankyou Music

iii. Chris Burns, *Pioneers of His Presence* (Chris Burns, 2014), ch. 7